Desktop Mastering

music PRO
guides

Desktop Mastering

Steve Turnidge

Hal Leonard Books

An Imprint of Hal Leonard Corporation

Published in 2012 by Hal Leonard Books
An Imprint of Hal Leonard Corporation
7777 West Bluemound Road
Milwaukee, WI 53213

Trade Book Division Editorial Offices
33 Plymouth St., Montclair, NJ 07042

Book design by Rainbow Tiger Design

Printed in the United States of America

Library of Congress Cataloging-in-Publication Data

Turnidge, Steve.
    Desktop mastering / Steve Turnidge.
        p. cm.
    Includes index.
    1. Mastering (Sound recordings) 2. Computer sound processing. I. Title.
    ML74.3.T87 2012
    781.3'4—dc23
                                                    2011045884
ISBN 978-1-4584-0374-2

www.halleonardbooks.com

Contents

Preface   ix

CHAPTER 1: A Conceptual Overview of Desktop Mastering   1
  Shoulders of Giants—The Path to the Present   2
  The External Mastering Chain   2
  The Desktop Mastering Chain   3
  Desktop Mastering Chain Functional Component Stages   4
    First Stage: Low-End Frequency Control   4
    Second Stage: Noise Reduction   4
    Third Stage: Stereo Enhancement   4
    Fourth Stage (optional): Reverb   5
    Fifth Stage (occasional): De-essing   5
    Sixth Stage: Multiband Compression, Expansion, and Equalization   5
    Seventh Stage: Look-ahead Limiting, Quantization, Noise Shaping,
      and Dither   6
    Eighth Stage: Visual Analysis   7
  The Bundle of Functionality   7
    Buggy Whips and Beyond   7

CHAPTER 2: The Listening Environment   9
  Tuning the Ear   9
  The Playback/Listening Chain   10
  Noise Colors   11
  The Flattening Procedure   11
  Room EQ   14
  Monitor Speaker Types   14
  Listening Levels   16
  Visual Feedback   16
  The Computer Working Environment   17
    Backups   17
    Software Applications   18

CHAPTER 3: Digital Audio Concepts   19
  Watches and Digital Audio   19
  Sampling   19
    Sample Rate   20
    Spectral Images   20
    Aliasing   21
    What Else Can Go Wrong?   22
    Bit Depth   22
  The Flipbook   23
    Time   23
    Resolution   24
    Choices   24

CHAPTER 4: Mixing for Mastering   25

Mixing Is Time Domain; Mastering Is Frequency Domain   25

The Sound Pyramid: Artistic Rules   26

Three Functional Rules   27

Should You Include Start and End Fades in Mixing?   31

Horror Stories   32

Multiple Versions   39

Name Your Files Logically   39

Do Things in the Right Order   41

File-Name Conventions   48

Preflight Checklist   48

Premaster Transport   48

YouSendIt   48

Dropbox   49

SoundCloud   49

CHAPTER 5: The Mastering Process   51

Receiving the Premaster   51

Prepare for Mastering   51

The Start Noise   52

Generate a Default Plug-in Chain for the Project   55

CHAPTER 6: The Desktop Mastering Chain   57

Get Them While They're Young: The Waves LinEQ Lowband   57

DC Offset Explained   59

Back to Setting the LinEQ Low Band   62

Keep Them Quiet: Noise Reduction   62

How Noise Reduction Algorithms Work   62

Noise Reduction Threshold Setting   64

Tuning the Noiseprint   65

The Reversal Trick: Reverse Noise Reduction   66

Special Purposes Fixes   67

Add a Dimension: The Waves S1 Stereo Imager   68

Becoming Centered   69

Mid-side Processing   70

Solving Stereo Phase Issues   70

Shuffling   71

Leveraging the Chain   71

Get a Room: Reverb   71

Stop the Sibilance: The Waves Renaissance DeEsser   72

How to Find Sibilant Frequencies   74

Balance and Strengthen: The Waves C4 Multiband

Parametric Processor   76

The C4 Frequency Ranges   77

Calibrating Ballistics, Vectors, and Dynamics   78

Make Everything MORE: The Waves L3 Ultramaximizer 82
Quantization, Dither, and Noise Shaping 83
Watch What You're Doing: The Waves PAZ Analyzer 86
Postmastering Processes 86
Cleanup: Tops and Tails 87
Tops 91
Tails 94
Fading Out Repeating Sections 96
The Human Lens 97
Mastered File Management and Delivery 97

CHAPTER 7: Sequencing and Production Master CDs 99
Sequencing 99
Track Spacing and the Snap Game 99
ISRC Codes 101
A CD Architect 5.0 Cautionary Tale 103
Sequencing Workflow 103

CHAPTER 8: Real World Mastering Applications 105
Options and Opportunities 105
Capture and Master Your Favorite Records and Tapes 106
Music Programs in High Schools and Colleges 106
Teen Center Studios 107
Professional Compilation Albums 107
Tribute Albums and Burning Sky Records 109
Greatest Hits and Career Overview Box Sets 110
Genealogy Transcriptions 111
Forensics 111
Companion CDs for Books and Instruction Manuals 111
Other Record Label Work 112
Seattle Fireworks Audio 112
Fireworks Cutdowns 118
Your Client and Opportunity Bases Are Infinite 121

CHAPTER 9: Mastering as a Business 123
The Business Bundle of Functionality 124
Begin Where You Are 124
Learn to Fail Fast 124
Generate and Cultivate a Brand 125
The Business Card 126
The Business Card Binder 128
Use QR Codes (or their current equivalent) 128
Stay Informed 128
Starting a Business 129
Business Insurance 129
Mileage and Travel 130
Keep a Lab Notebook 130

Money   131
Invoicing   131
The Client Environment   132
Client Contact and Recruitment   132
Client Communications   132
Marketing Methods   133
The Four-Foot Forks   133
The Talent Tarot   134
Self-Employment   134
The Social Graph   135
Use Social Networks as Performance Spaces   135
Life Streaming   136
Status Messages   136
Be Everywhere at Once   136
Use Social Networks at Their "Sharp End"   137
Comments Are Currency   137
Planning Ahead and Goal Setting   138

CHAPTER 10: Fundamentals of Audio   139
The Ocean of Air   139
Propagation   140
The Waveform Explained   143
Units of Measurement: the Decibel (dB)   146
Everything Is Relative   147
Characteristics of a Wave   147

CHAPTER 11: An Introduction to Electricity and Electronics   153
Electricity   154
Electronic Components   156
Filters   158
Crossovers   159
Signal Processor Families   159
Amplitude Processors   159
Frequency Processors   161
Frequency and Amplitude Processors   161
Time-Based Processors   163
Major Components   164
The Amplifier   164

CHAPTER 12: Conclusion   167
Multidimensional Vision   167
Windup   168

Audio Taxonomy: A Glossary of Subtle Terms   171
UltraViolet Studios Discography   173
Acknowledgments   183
The *Desktop Mastering* Companion DVD-ROM   185
Index   193

Preface

Mastering your music is like mastering your life. It's amazing what happens when you clean up the noise, maximize your good work, and have your music sparkle and shine the way you really want it to.

Welcome to *Desktop Mastering*! This book describes the tools and methods I use every day to maintain a comfortable existence with desktop mastering at its core, including the broader issues of personal networking, marketing, and taking care of business. The tools I describe are not as important as the techniques, which are transferrable to any rendition of current technological offerings.

Some of the ideas presented here may initially strike you as unlikely. That is a good thing—it's the first of three stages of acceptance that tend to go something like this:

1. "You're crazy, that'll never work—give up now!"
2. "I know that exists, but I have no use for it."
3. "Of course that's how you do it! What took you so long?!"

So, in my business and dealings, when I hear "That will never work!" from others, I smile to myself and understand that they have reached the first stage of acceptance.

In this book, you'll learn the specific processes I've developed over the past decade to successfully and consistently master audio fully in the box (without external processing equipment). *Desktop Mastering* also covers all the basics you'll need to know to understand what the mastering engineer needs from a mix, with specific advice regarding how to set up your listening environment and what is needed to provide an optimal premaster. Included in the companion DVD-ROM are real-world examples of premastered files and their mastered counterparts for you to practice on in your own studio.

You'll find chapters that will introduce you to the fundamentals of digital and analog audio and electronics, which provides a great starting point and directions for further study.

Finally, there are sections on practical and pragmatic methods to apply what you've learned. Not only can you master your own music, but it might be time for you to start offering your mastering services to others as well, with the potential of having your own business doing what you love.

A Conceptual Overview of Desktop Mastering

There are three types of mastering—cosmetic, aesthetic, and restorative—just as in dentistry.

- Cosmetic dentistry is used to make shiny, brilliant teeth that stand out in a crowd and look great in smiles walking up the red carpet.
- Aesthetic dentistry is used to match the nearby teeth to make the set appear to be a whole—the work looking natural, as if it were meant to be that way.
- Restorative dentistry brings back into order the functionally incorrect—removing unpleasant and dysfunctional aspects, while adding what is necessary to restore the patient to full health.

In mastering, you have the opportunity to provide similar services to your clients.

- Electronica, hip-hop, rock, and pop can sparkle and shine, and rise above the crowd with cosmetic mastering.
- Jazz, classical, and location recording benefit from aesthetic presentation in a clear and unadorned way, accurately portraying the performances without distraction.
- Forensics and archival mastering restores damaged and noisy sources to intelligible carriers of information. Sometimes, the archival restoration is the first step, to be followed by a cosmetic or aesthetic stage for final presentation.

Shoulders of Giants—The Path to the Present

Historically, mastering has been a process of transformation, typically from one medium of information storage to another. Throughout most of mastering's history, the goal behind it was to physically lathe vibration forms into the groove of a disc. This process required significant skill and craft, and the pool of accomplished mastering engineers was limited. A series of tools were at the mastering engineer's disposal, specifically purpose-built to inscribe the most delicate of details onto the production master disc, which would be the template for thousands of commercially released duplications of it. Mastering then evolved with the introduction of the cassette tape, which had its own limitations to be finessed.

Finally, with the introduction of the compact disc, the age of digital mastering was upon us. The mastering engineers had a substantial learning curve to overcome—the finesse needed to eke out the finest details from vinyl (and the tricks required to do so) did not translate well at first to the CD.

RIAA Equalization

One of the tricks used to keep phonograph styli in the groove was a frequency equalization process called the RIAA Curve, which reduces low frequencies (that would toss the stylus around) and increases high frequencies (to capture the sound in finer detail). Phonograph preamplifiers have a complementary (equal and opposite) filter curve built in to boost the low frequencies and reduce high-frequency content, with the benefit of reduced hiss but the liability of higher rumble.

Some of the earliest transfers to CD retained the aspects of this earlier technology, resulting in a lack of low end and a brittle high end. Over a period of time, experience had its way, and the mastering industry found its niche—and the age of the CD eclipsed all the media that had come before.

The External Mastering Chain

The one consistent thread among mastering engineers up until the late 1980s (and beyond) was that they all used functional components chained together to do their job. The use, order, and settings of these components were the distinguishing factors among mastering engineers.

The mastering process has been transformed by technological and computational evolution. This shift is from "out of the box" (which is something of a misnomer, since there are many boxes used in external mastering chains), toward "in the box," or desktop mastering—where the full processing functionality of the mastering chain is controlled and applied inside a desktop computer. The majority of mastering engineers at the time of this writing employ a hybrid system, typically running a number of processes with outboard gear while bringing the premastered audio into their digital environment. The *desktop mastering chain* has developed and evolved fully in the box for more than a decade, and is what I have to share with you.

There is at least one overlapping requirement regardless of where the processing lies: an appropriate and accurate reproduction chain is necessary to inform the choices at the heart of the mastering process. Being able to hear what you are doing and knowing what to do are at the core of mastering.

The Desktop Mastering Chain

The real focus of this book is the concept of the *bundle of functionality*, which, in desktop mastering, is a specific and functional chain of plug-in processors within a digital audio workstation environment. The functionality of the whole is a synergetic superset of each individual processor.

All mastering (and audio, for that matter) boils down to only two aspects—frequency and level. The primary function of any mastering chain is to balance frequencies and provide the desired level in each channel, whether it is a slamming highly compressed signal or a delicate, quiet passage.

The desktop mastering chain can be realized with any number of tools from different providers. You don't have to use my specific chain. Finding what works for you in your situation is the fun part, and that is one of the reasons I'll go into detail about my specific setup—it is what works for me. Taking a journey of discovery often leads to finding new ways of solving old problems, and distinguishing yourself as a provider of a unique service at the same time.

Desktop Mastering Chain Functional Component Stages

Setting up the desktop mastering chain, as in sculptural technique, begins with crude moves to bring the audio file into a generally balanced frequency spectrum, with levels optimized for the next stages in the chain.

First Stage: Low-End Frequency Control

The minimal functionality needed for this first stage is a highpass filter set at 20 Hz, a general level control, and some low-frequency equalization.

The prime function of this first stage is to minimize potentially uncontrolled energy in the low end. Low-frequency energy is often out of balance, and literally takes up the most room of any waveform. Taming it here allows the rest of the chain to have the most headroom possible for its processes.

Second Stage: Noise Reduction

The next stage is low-level noise reduction used to expand the dynamic range of the material (the difference between the loudest and the softest sounds in the file). Ideally the noise reduction stage has a frequency-setting component that allows shaping of the reduction threshold curve, the tuning of which is required for excellent overall results. This stage is like washing the windows—you may not realize how bad they were until they're clean.

Third Stage: Stereo Enhancement

Now that the low frequencies are controlled and the noise floor has been dropped, it is time to provide subtle stereo enhancement. The processor in this stage provides overall stereo phase and channel balancing control, as well as a method to widen the soundstage. These actions are all taken before turning the level up (or *taking gain*), which happens a couple of stages down the road.

Gain staging is a critical concept: a properly gain-staged chain of processor levels are set so that any clipping that occurs on the first processor simultaneously clips the rest of the chain. This ensures the maximum headroom and dynamic range for the entire chain.

In contrast, if the output of one stage is set at a very quiet level, and the next stage has to have its input turned way up to compensate, what you are actually turning up is the noise present in both stages. The better way to set gain is to have outputs set as loudly as possible without clipping the next stage; that way, the input can be set very low and still provide sufficient and necessary volume without turning up unnecessary noise.

Fourth Stage (optional): Reverb

Very rarely, a track comes in that is dry as a bone, and it practically scrapes as it travels through the plug-in chain. In these cases, and at this stage of the chain, I'll provide some very subtle and light reverb, just enough to restore the illusion that there are people playing together in a room. I've had to use reverb in this way perhaps five times out of more than 200 projects.

Fifth Stage (occasional): De-essing

The de-esser provides a complementary function to the first low-frequency control stage, only for high frequencies. The explicit purpose of this stage is to set up the high end for the next stage, controlling *ess* and *sh* sounds, and leveling out the top octaves for upper-midrange expansion.

Sixth Stage: Multiband Compression, Expansion, and Equalization

This stage may be a bit challenging to emulate. I use a Waves C4 Multiband Parametric Processor, which provides four bands of compression/expansion, plus dynamic equalization. Previously, I used a 10-band EQ and a 4-band multiband dynamics processor to take care of the issues that this single processor solves.

This is the stage where you need to balance the frequency range with a high level of detail. The coarse aspects of the file have been smoothed out previously in the chain, and now it is time to provide kick and punch to the track. The low end of the multiband compressor has a very fast attack and release, allowing the kick drum and bass to be dynamic and moving.

The most critical section of the entire chain is the upper midrange of this stage, the residence of articulation. This section is where the signal, having been conditioned by the de-esser, is expanded and requires much finer control—tenths of a decibel make significant changes here. Like a series of levers, the stages are amplified in very noticeable steps at this stage. The earlier stages, if bypassed, are extremely subtle, providing general direction to the sound, as compared with the processing here.

The main secret of all of these stages up to and including this point is to make the file absolutely neutral, so that nothing sticks out and all is smooth and clear. The reason this is important is because the look-ahead limiter is coming up next.

Seventh Stage: Look-ahead Limiting, Quantization, Noise Shaping, and Dither

This is the culmination of the chain—everything that has been set up to this point has been specifically tuned to be presented to the final limiter. This is a stage that is commonly misused, and *is* misused if it is applied significantly prior to this very last stage. When premasters are subjected to brickwall limiters and hard compression, the job of the mastering engineer becomes one of restoration. Compression in all its forms, while useful as a tool, can be devastating as a weapon. This stage makes everything MORE. If there is sibilance or boominess, they are aggravated here.

The other critical functions provided by this stage are quantization, dither, and noise shaping. *Quantization* is the intelligent reduction in bit depth from (typically) 24 bit to 16 bit. The wrong way to quantize is called *truncation*, which is just chopping off the last eight bits of the digital word. Using intelligent quantization, together with a distortion reducing technique called *dither*, provides a file ready to be released on CD.

Noise shaping gathers unavoidable digital noise (a result of digital signal processing) and mathematically moves the noise to the highest audible frequencies, generally around 18 or 19 kHz. This also is a function which *must* be done last. The next digital process on the file collapses the noise back out to the whole frequency range, while leaving the previous noise shaping heap up at the top of the range.

This presents us with an object lesson: tools, if used incorrectly, can leave a bad taste and give a lasting (and potentially wrong) opinion regarding the utility of the tool. For instance, if you pour a big mound of salt in your hand and throw it into your mouth, you are likely to have a lasting distaste for salt. However, in cooking we smell the delicate differences within the food and determine "too much of this, not enough of that" and balance it out—in which case, salt is a necessity. As mastering engineers, our job is to listen and perceive the flavors of the sound and modify the recipe to match the ingredients. In the end, the track has the potential to be delicious.

Eighth Stage: Visual Analysis

Never operate without an X-ray. This is the visual representation of your work, and you should have a phase display and a frequency display. In addition to a software analyzer, I recommend you have and constantly use a hardware real-time analyzer to observe the balance and motion of the sound.

The Bundle of Functionality

The key to the bundle of functionality is interchangeable functions. With this key, you can take the feature descriptions and context of each plug-in and transfer them to current technological offerings.

Buggy Whips and Beyond

The bundle of functionality can conceptually be likened to an automobile—a functional device made up of specific subfunctional devices in specific relationships to each other.

The turn of the 21st century was the dawn of the digital-media era. At that time we discussed the fate of the music industry in terms of the buggy-whip industry of a century before, which was destined for extinction as a result of not accepting reality and therefore being unable to change with the times.

We are still on that 100-year interval with the current condition of the music-sales ecosystem. Now we are similar to the nascent automotive industry of the early 20th century. The major components of automotive systems were defined by then—motors, tires, steering wheels, chassis, tailpipes, and so on.

In the earliest days of automobile design and evolution, components were defined and placed into their context with other components. Wheels attach to axles, axles attach to chassis, engines and steering wheels in their proper places. At some point, the contextual functionality of each piece was well defined; critical systems manufacturers could go out of business without destroying the entire industry because the system components had been defined in a context relative to the rest of the bundle of functionality that made up an automobile. It became generally known what a wheel was and the function it needed to perform. Separated from context, however, it wasn't nearly as useful. Sitting with a tire in your lap will get you nowhere fast!

Each component in the system became upgradable to provide a better fit, function, and efficiency in context of the whole. This created opportunities for innovators who were working toward the goal of making better overall systems.

The components of an automobile, when taken separately, are minimally functional toward the aim of arriving at a given destination. But applied in context, they afford the luxury of arriving at nearly any identifiable goal or destination. Replaceable parameters enable the bundle of functionality, and you will see the value of replaceable parameters repeatedly in this book.

2

The Listening Environment

You will most likely begin your mastering career in a residence. It is possible to set up a system to reproduce audio accurately enough to make decisions about what you are hearing (which is at the core of both mixing and mastering processes), but you first need to understand how to listen, and the distinction between hearing and listening. If you can hear, you hear all the time—it is a built-in safety mechanism to help us avoid predators and other dangers. Listening, on the other hand, requires consciousness and attention.

Tuning the Ear

Here is a good listening exercise: sit in "silence" at your workstation. Now, listen to the sounds around you; listen to and hear your computers, air-conditioning, neighbors, street noise, birds. Then, listen farther than you can hear—extend your senses. This is a good starting point for your audio work.

I had the good fortune to have been in Seattle during the run of the Guitar Craft location-based music series spin-off called Tuning the Air. These weekly performances consist of 8 to 12 acoustic guitarists playing in a circle around the audience. I am the designated audient; my role in the performances is to pay attention and listen, even if there are no other people in the audience. This is what transforms the Tuning the Air ensemble's "practice" into a "performance."

Tuning the Air

To date, I've attended more than 200 Tuning the Air performances over seven years. It has become quite a learning and transformative experience from the listening perspective. Being surrounded by sound is interesting in this context, but the real lesson is that we are always surrounded by sound, and it is the amount of concentrated attention we bring to the experience that fuels the transformation.

Seek out experiential listening opportunities; just know that you may be disappointed by audience chatter in most of them. This process of sharpening your listening attention is a critical exercise toward becoming a superb audio professional.

The Playback/Listening Chain

Mastering in the box has eliminated much of the equipment-interconnection and impedance-matching issues that were critical items in earlier mastering days.

Here is the typical desktop mastering playback chain:

Computer > Audio Interface > Signal Processing > Amplifier > Speakers

This book was written during a stage of technology in which computers and audio interfaces are generally commodity items. Any new versions of these devices are generally superior to past products. The benefit is to be able to focus on what really does matter—the speakers and your relationship with them in the room.

Different types of speakers do sound different, and sometimes older models and versions are superior to current models. There are two functions you'll need to perform to get accurate playback: first, there is listening, and second, there is flattening your system with a real-time analyzer. I also recommend having a subwoofer.

I am very fortunate to have a mastering room upstairs in my house that is under a steep roof. The ceiling corners are cut on the long axis a third of the way down the walls, and there is a door in the opposite corner of the room from my monitoring area that has a staircase leading down which behaves as a big port for the room—the low frequencies have a place to escape.

This is not a perfect listening environment from every spot in the room (the couch behind the mastering station has a lot of boomy bass present), but in the sweet spot, close to and in a triangular relationship with near-field speakers, the frequency response is very accurate. I call it the beach ball–sized sweet spot—just big enough for my head to fit in. If a client wants to hear something accurately (and be able to make a decision), I invite him or her into the sweet spot.

I use JBL 4208 monitors with titanium dome tweeters and a JBL LSR4312SP subwoofer, with the audio going through a Rane RPM-2 for room EQ to flatten the frequency response at the listening position (which I highly recommend).

Noise Colors

One of the best ways to ensure that the audio coming out of your speakers and hitting your ears matches what went into the system is to "flatten the room." The language used to perform this function is the language of noise. Certain types of noise have the appropriate energy at appropriate frequencies to be able to help ensure as much transparency from your system as possible.

Different flavors of noise are named after different flavors of visible light, and the wavelengths that make up the light. *White noise*, like white light, has equal energy at each frequency in the audio spectrum. This means that the 10,000 frequencies in the top octave (between 10 kHz and 20 kHz) have the same amount of energy as the rest of the audio spectrum from 20 Hz to 10 kHz, making for some pretty high-frequency noise!

In light, the longer wavelengths (lower frequencies) are red shifted, so noise content that weighs toward the lower frequencies are called *red noise* or *brown noise*, which are used more in oceanography. *Black noise* is full silence.

The most useful noise for our purposes is called *pink noise*, and it features constant power per octave, as compared with constant power per frequency. This is the type of noise used for the room-flattening procedure.

The Flattening Procedure

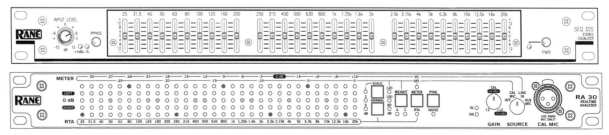

Preflattened State

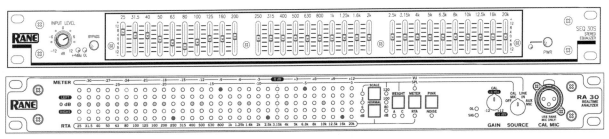

Setting the EQ

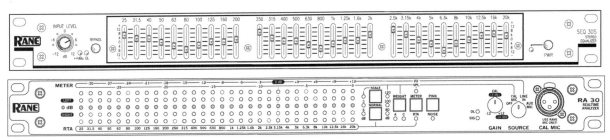

The Final EQ Curve

"Flattening" a room is done using a real-time analyzer (RTA). The process is to take pink noise (often generated by the RTA), put it through your audio system and your speakers, and pick up the resulting sound with a calibrated, flat microphone as input into the RTA. The signal picked up by the microphone is interpreted into a visual display that reads out the energy received in (generally) one-third-octave regions, matching the controls on a one-third-octave equalizer. Using the RTA display, the system is calibrated by raising and lowering the EQ at each band until the signal received by the microphone matches the signal being injected into the system. The signal flow to flatten the room is the following: Pink noise out of the RTA > Preamp > EQ > Amp > Speakers > RTA Microphone > RTA Mic input.

When you listen to different speaker systems, you are listening to more than just the speakers—you are listening to whole systems. One big surprise I had a few years ago was to buy new powered monitors and a new subwoofer, and find out that I couldn't hear the specific upper midrange articulation frequencies that I tune in to in order to master. I then went through the motions of flattening with an RTA, but those frequencies were just not being replicated. These new speakers used a silk dome tweeter, and what I had replaced used a titanium dome tweeter. In my case, the metal in the tweeter appeared to make a difference. This also points out the limitation of flattening "at the listening position": if the speakers do not put out the frequencies you need to hear, no amount of signal processing will solve that problem. When flattening works, it's like taking blankets off the speakers. There should be a distinct and positive change between the EQ in the system and the bypassed EQ.

The curves for my system are shown in the first figure below, and a detail of the curve in shown in the second figure. These images show the Rane DragNet software that controls my Rane RPM-2—a very useful device.

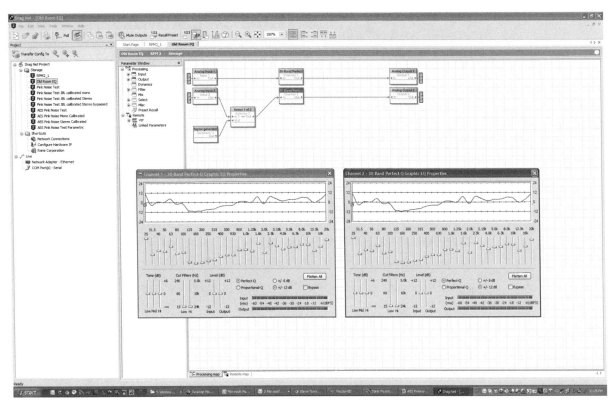

Rane DragNet EQ Setup

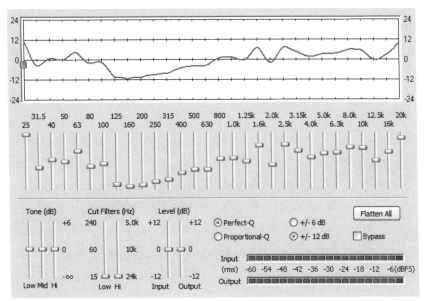

Room EQ Detail

Room EQ

The location in the signal chain where EQ is applied is critical and, if incorrect, can result in pretty serious errors. It is important that the EQ settings go only to your amps and speakers, and are not set within your workstation software to be added to your work's output. This should be pretty obvious but is important to specify—room EQ is just for the room, not for your audio material under edit. Another challenge is that it is possible to set up a configuration of an EQ going straight into an amp without a level control on a preamp, or that the level control on your audio interface may not always work (if the computer is off, for instance). This can result in damaging levels, and with some audio interfaces that are USB powered without power switches, very loud thuds and bangs are generated during boot-up. When designing your system, keep your level control location and functionality in mind.

Monitor Speaker Types

There are several monitor speaker types, defined by where your ears are in relationship with the speakers. Typically they fall into two categories: far-field and near-field, with some specialized variants.

Far-field monitors are larger speakers with (generally) broader frequency response than near-fields. Their distance permits a larger sweet spot, and they are well suited for tracking because of their full-range nature, and more than one person at a time can enjoy accurate sound. However, because of their distance from the engineer, the signal often interacts and is colored with reflections from the room. Far-field speaker systems usually require quite a lot of acoustic treatment to provide the best sound to the largest area. In larger studios, they are often built into wall soffits to increase efficiency and reduce reflections. When flattening a room with EQ (as described above), far-field monitors require separate EQ curves for each speaker.

Near-field monitors, on the other hand, are used to allow access to the direct signal from speakers, without reflection from console or other surfaces. Near-field monitoring creates a very narrow sweet spot—the speakers and your ears should form an equilateral triangle, with the high-frequency drivers at ear level. Current near-field monitors are accurate enough to make far-fields not as necessary, but they are appropriate for just a single decision maker to use at a time. In my room, clients have to come into the sweet spot to make suggestions—no suggestions from the couch.

EQ near-field speakers with the same curve for each speaker (left and right), otherwise the stereo imaging breaks down horribly. The lack of accurate very low frequency response in near-field monitors suggests the addition of a subwoofer, which I highly recommend. When you do have a subwoofer, use *bass management*; this is a term taken from surround sound systems, in which the subwoofer is considered part of the stereo speakers rather than as a low-frequency effects (LFE) separate channel.

Bass Management and Surround Sound

Surround sound systems are typically more difficult to configure than stereo, especially if you need a fully accurate playback system. The room must be acoustically dead and nearly quadrilaterally symmetrical (square), and the sweet spot is generally very small. I have mixed and mastered some surround sound content (for a wristwatch advertisement), but I did it on my stereo workstation, burning the results to DVD and checking out the results in my home theater. This was a challenge (the year was around 2005), and I've not taken more jobs like it. One of the main problems I ran into was that the mastering chain was specifically two channels. I had to split out the left/right, left rear/right rear, and center/LFE channels in stereo; master them separately; and recombine them in Sony Vegas to generate the surround-encoded DVD. The work did pay off—the spot had international exposure and was nominated for an advertising award—but the process was just a bit too convoluted for my taste.

Another important monitoring environment is your car stereo. I've been fortunate to have a very nice stock stereo system in my car of the past decade, and find it to be a great check on my work. One time I had a bit of a shock, however. I received a disc back from a band after CD production, and I was quite excited to hear it. I popped it into the car player, and all of a sudden the bass was *way* too much. This is always a concern (finding issues *after* the CD is made). Fortunately, I realized that I had recently had the car serviced, and the technicians had boosted the bass EQ all the way up on the stereo. Returning the levels to flat solved the issue, and I was relieved and happy.

This brings up a point about what your clients hear in different environments, and with different hearing abilities. It is interesting to get feedback from the different members of a band—often the drummer will comment on the level not being loud enough. You can generally tell if a member of a self-produced band mixed their album, because you'll hear a lot of that particular member's parts. Guitarists and bass players are famous for this.

Listening Levels

Equal Loudness Contours

Find a good level for playback, and calibrate your ear to it. Physiologically, for small rooms, 79 dB SPL is the optimal level for the most even balance of your hearing. Below 79 dB highs are emphasized and above 79 dB lows are emphasized. At soft levels, your hearing becomes less sensitive to low frequencies. The reason for this is that if your hearing were highly sensitive to low-level low frequencies, hearing your heartbeat and blood flow in your body would drive you nuts. Likewise, the most sensitive parts of your hearing are between 2 and 3 kHz, the realm of whispers. See the QR code on the left for more information.

Visual Feedback

As important as the audio presentation is in order to make appropriate decisions, the visual aspect is critical as well. Having a good-sized, high-resolution video monitor is recommended, and fortunately these have become quite inexpensive.

Most video cards now have at least two DVI outputs. This provides an opportunity that has served me very well—to have a client video monitor. This is a second monitor duplicating your primary work monitor, but it's over your shoulder for your client to watch.

Video monitoring of a running waveform is one of several methods to see a waveform transformed into a visual representation, and one of the most dynamic. Watching an audio waveform travel by at a 16:1 zoom level is educational—the color density reflects the frequencies represented. As you watch the waveforms go by, note what sibilance and boominess look like: low frequencies are big and open, bright dense parts are high frequencies, really bright bits are sibilance.

Another monitoring option I highly recommend is having a real-time analyzer with a graphic display of the entire frequency range. This also can be very educational—sometimes frequencies are represented that you may not hear, giving you an opportunity for detective work.

The Computer Working Environment

Your efficiency operating and navigating your digital audio workstation software directly translates into your ability to generate an income from that activity. If you are currently unfamiliar with the basics and keyboard shortcuts of your DAW, you have a great opportunity to enhance your efficiency.

I use a Logitech G13 macro game board to make shortcuts for many of my high-production software environments, from mastering to PCB design to just launching programs.

Logitech G13 Settings

The minimum number of keyboard shortcuts you should learn and use include the following:

- Save
- Save As
- Go to home (beginning of file)
- Increase level magnification
- Decrease level magnification
- Increase time magnification (zoom in)
- Decrease time magnification (zoom out)
- Play or stop the contents of the data window
- Pause playback and leave the cursor at the current position
- Go to next track
- Go to previous track

Once you've found out how easy it is to use keyboard shortcuts (once you learn them), you may find that most of your repetitive work can be somewhat automated. The G13, for instance, has a macro recorder in it that lets you assign a key to any number of moves; this is great for commands that are normally embedded deeply in the program's menuing systems. The rule is to be very good at navigation. It looks more professional to your clients as well!

Backups

Data is transient and fragile. Back up your work often, and always have at least two copies (in different places) of critical files. In addition, have a clear enough filing system to be able to find work from several years in the past. Be consistent in your file-naming and directory structures.

Have a backup of your operating system drive good enough that you could rebuild and be back in business within a day or two. The enhanced data technologies of cloud computing are making this step much less arduous.

Software Applications

One thing that is consistent in this business is change, especially on the software front. Most software updates and upgrades are purchased online and downloaded. It is a good idea to print out the receipts with your serial numbers and user names (store passwords separately) for all your different software, and keep them in a three-ring binder. Protect it well—that is an expensive binder!

I keep a program updates directory that has a subdirectory for each software company I deal with, and I download the latest updates to their individual directories. If you have cloud storage, your program updates directory is probably a good candidate to be backed up there. I ran into difficulty when a hard drive crashed, and it was the one that had both my program updates and all my e-mail with the serial numbers on it. That is when I learned to print my receipts out—it saves both time and money!

3

Digital Audio Concepts

Before I go into detail about mixing for mastering, let's get a good handle on digital audio in general—then you can make informed decisions regarding your medium.

Watches and Digital Audio

There are two kinds of clocks we are familiar with: analog and digital.

An analog watch sweeps through every point between the numbers on the face of the dial. A digital watch jumps from number to number discretely. Digital audio transforms analog waveforms to numbers that can be expressed as a series of on or off, one or zero (binary) signals. Once you have decided to convert something into numbers, you have a choice. How many numbers, and of what range?

RaneNote 137: Digital Dharma of Audio A/D Converters

This is the domain of *analog-to-digital converters* (ADC) and of their central function, which is quantization. *Quantization* means to make something into numbers. The prefix *quant* means "number," or "quantity"; the suffix *ization* means *to make* (for instance, *mechanization* means to "make mechanical").

Sampling

One way that an analog-to-digital converter transcribes continuous analog voltages into discrete numerical values is through a process called successive approximation. There have been several other strategies developed to capture digital audio over time; this is one of the early methods, and serves our purposes for understanding this process.

A continuously varying signal is measured against a clock and is held steady at each clock tick (this happens very quickly). During each sample period, for each 'bit,' the input voltage is compared (using a comparator) with a given voltage, beginning with the midpoint of the sample range—defining the most significant bit. The first voltage you are comparing against is the value corresponding to the speaker at rest, or air pressure in the room. If the incoming signal voltage is greater than this voltage, the bit position gets a one. If the signal is smaller, a zero is logged.

You've just determined whether this voltage is positive or negative (or, put another way, whether the speaker will be moving out or in during this sample). Let's say the value is found to be positive—the most significant bit position gets a binary 1 value. Next, for the same sample period, set the comparator halfway up the positive range, and ask the question again: Is the voltage being measured higher or lower than this new comparison value? If it is above the midpoint of the positive swing, log a binary 1 in the second bit position; if below, assign a binary 0. Now reset your comparison point to the middle of the range you just discovered, and ask the question again. Repeat 16 times total for 16-bit word length, 24 times for 24-bit. You just made a sample!

Now, release that voltage and grab the next one at the next clock tick and repeat (all the above happens for each sample).

Sample Rate

Cool. That's what happens during each clock cycle to generate samples. But how do you decide how fast to run your clock? How many samples per second have to be taken to accurately represent and be able to reproduce the waveform? Fortunately, someone figured that out—his name was Harry Nyquist (1889–1976). The Nyquist theorem states that a signal must be sampled at least twice as fast as the bandwidth of the signal to accurately reconstruct the waveform; otherwise, the high-frequency content will alias at a frequency inside the spectrum of interest (the passband). Since you'd like to accurately capture the entire audio-frequency spectrum, of which the highest frequency is 20 kHz, this implies a theoretical minimum sample rate of twice that rate, or 40 kHz.

Spectral Images

As usual, there is a bit of a twist. In digital signal processing there are "ghosts" called *spectral images*, and their locations are defined by the sample rate. The higher the sample rate, the farther away the spectral images are separated from each other, occurring at multiples of the sampling frequency. Just as in the movie *Ghostbusters*, if you cross a spectral image with your audio, phantom waveforms are generated, producing what is called *aliasing*.

Here's where the spectral images come from: the signal spectrum is the passband you wish to sample. In audio that would be 20 Hz to 20 kHz, which you can consider being on the "right-hand side" of 0 Hz. In sampling theory, you imaginarily mirror the passband around 0 Hz (on the "left-hand side"), making a mirror image of the passband.

The passband and its mirror image are collectively called a *spectrum image*. When you have determined a sample rate (frequency), copy the spectrum image to center on that frequency. Additionally, create copies of the spectral images at even multiples of the sample rate all the way up the frequency range.

The key to avoiding aliasing is to keep the spectral images from overlapping. An anti-aliasing filter is a lowpass filter that filters out higher-frequency spectral images. Anti-aliasing filters have various cutoff slopes—fast rolloff or slow rolloff. The steeper the cutoff slope of a filter, the more ripple in the passband (needless to say, a flat passband is preferred).

Where does that leave us with the 40 kHz sample rate? The spectral image is shoved right up against 20 kHz in that case, without any room to place an anti-aliasing filter. So, the compact disc and digital-audio standard sampling rate was set at 44.1 kHz, specifically to push the spectral image up by a few kilohertz and allow for a reasonable (but still steep) anti-aliasing filter.

Aliasing

You've found out that crossing spectral images is a bad thing, but what does it really cause? The figure below shows a 7 kHz signal sampled at 8 kHz, and the resulting sample points marked by the intersections of the sampled waveform on the sample-rate grid. The reconstruction of this high frequency is obviously incorrect—it is a waveform aliasing, or pretending to be, the correct frequency. Aliasing errors exist in the captured data, not the reconstruction. An 8 kHz sample rate should not be given any frequencies above 4 kHz, or this kind of thing will be the result. A high frequency, sampled at too low a rate, looks like a lower-frequency signal.

Aliasing

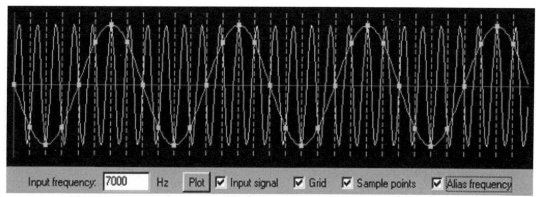

Input frequency: 7000 Hz | Plot | ☑ Input signal ☑ Grid ☑ Sample points ☑ Alias frequency

A 7 kHz Signal Sampled at 8 kHz

What Else Can Go Wrong?

Now that you have determined to take samples 44,100 times a second, it is important that those samples are accurately spaced; otherwise, when the digital numbers are put back into an analog waveform, distortion results. An improper spacing of the sample rate is called *jitter*. Once jitter is introduced into the conversion, there is no way to correct for it.

Bit Depth

As a mastering engineer, my 16-bit masters sound significantly superior to the 24-bit mixes I begin with, but it's important for me to start with the 24-bit files. Digital audio has time resolution (measured in samples) and amplitude resolution (determined by bit depth). I highly prefer better amplitude resolution than higher sample rates.

First of all, according to the Nyquist theorem, the frequency band from 20 Hz to 20 kHz is amply served by a 44.1 kHz sample rate. The only thing higher sample rates provide for are gentler sloping lowpass anti-aliasing filters above 20 kHz.

However, an increase in bit depth gives a measurable increase in quality and accuracy. If I receive a 16-bit premaster file, each sample has 65,536 different potential values, split in half (32,768 for the positive waveform, and 32,768 for the negative waveform). On the other hand, 24-bit files provide 16,777,216 values (8,388,608 for the positive waveform and 8,388,608 for the negative waveform).

When an analog-to-digital converter does its work, a voltage is converted into a digital word. Higher accuracy in the conversion produces less quantization distortion. I tell my clients the following story as an illustration of the comparison between 16- and 24-bit files:

- The distance between Seattle and Austin is 1,769 miles.
- Measured in 16-bit increments, that is one mark every 142 feet (65,536 total increments, 96 dB dynamic range).
- Measured in 24-bit increments, there is a mark every 6 inches (16,777,216 increments, 144 dB dynamic range).

Let's think up a little helper to get a handle on the idea of digital conversion—let's call him the Quantization Genie. It's his job to ultimately determine what numerical value to give to an analog measurement. When the Quantization Genie sees the voltage fall from the sky, he has to line it up with the nearest mark. With 16-bit, he has to run one way or the other up to 142 feet. With 24-bit, the voltage is calibrated within the nearest six inches—no running required; he can just drop it at his feet.

Looked at another way, a full-volume 16-bit file is equivalent to a 16-times-softer 24-bit file. So, when I get premaster files, I request 24-bit files with peaks that are 2 dB to 3 dB down from full scale. This provides what appears to be a quiet file, but with ten times more resolution than a maxed 16-bit file.

One of the last processors in the desktop mastering chain is a quantizer, a tool that selectively takes those (24-bit) six-inch increments and runs them out to the (16-bit) 142-foot marks. It works with a rule base called dither, which keeps the quantizer from going in the same direction too often. The mastering chain and its settings determine the amount of signal manipulation and compression that a mastered file has, but a 24-bit audio premaster source file always provides more resolution to work with.

The Flipbook

Here is another way to understand the relationship between sample rate and bit depth—with a thought experiment about dimensions and time.

Time

In an animated flipbook, the characters are flat. As you flip the book, they appear to have motion. If you stop flipping, pause, and start again, does the character notice? I think not, since time itself stopped for the character. Let's say the flipbook, and therefore the character's time, is calibrated to one-inch-worth of pages per second. (What if the flipbook character's time was calibrated to 44,100 pages per second? Or 48,000 pages per second?)

Each one of these pages can be equated with an individual sample position. This "flatland" flipbook character can know what an "inch" is, since he can measure out an inch-long line. You can tell the character, "If you rotate that inch orthogonally [at right angles] to everything you know, that is your time." The number of pages dedicated to generating the flipbook's motion in one second can be considered to be the sample rate. (As an aside, if the pages of the flipbook are recorded at any time that is other than at exactly spaced samples, then the playback, even if exactly spaced, will contain jitter).

Resolution

That's fine for the quickly turning pages of the flipbook, but what you are really interested in is the quality of the pictures on those pages. Are they sketched out in pencil, or are they lavish oil paintings, photographically accurate, or better? This is where the concept of bit rate kicks in.

Do you remember the evolution of computer video cards? In the early days of color computer video adapters, you had 8-bit video cards, which allowed for 256 colors. Time passed, and 16-bit video graphics adapters were introduced into the market, increasing the color palette to a total of 65,536 available colors. Eventually, the 24-bit Truecolor standard was released, for a total of 16,777,216 color variations. This same evolution in digital representation can be applied to sampling bit depths.

In our flipbooks, the images can be thought of as being made up with these different resolutions. For example, 8-bit audio allows for 256 levels of definition, 16-bit audio allows for 65,536 levels of resolution, and 24-bit audio allows for 16,777,216—millions of levels of resolution.

Choices

If you had the opportunity to select between a higher sample rate (the flipbook's speed resolution) and a higher image resolution, which would you prefer? Personally, I'd prefer to see the higher-resolution images, especially since the Nyquist theorem ensures sampling accuracy as long as the speed resolution is better than twice the highest speed flipbook action you are trying to capture, which in the digital audio domain a 44.1 kHz sample rate satisfies.

In closing this chapter, I hope you've gained a good respect for bit depth. When people tell me that they only have a premaster on an audio CD or have only recorded in 16-bit, I ask them to at least mix down to 24-bit if they can. This provides for a distinct (and reasonably easy) quality increase versus mixing down to 16-bit.

Mixing for Mastering

The mixing engineer's job is to take anywhere from three to several hundred tracks and mix them down to two tracks (or surround sound), ready for the mastering engineer. During this process the mix engineer has a broad palette of functions to apply and decisions to make.

Each of these actions is in the service of preparing the ideal premaster to send to the mastering engineer. The beneficiaries of a good mixing job are firstly the music, then the listener, then the artist, and lastly the mixing engineer, who will potentially earn repeat business from the job.

A necessary component of the process is to have a clear and positive relationship between the mixing engineer and the mastering engineer. This relationship is often rocky to begin with, but becomes really efficient once established. A good idea for an initial workflow is to send the *first* track of a new session to the mastering engineer for evaluation. This ensures that problems will be caught early, rework will be minimized, and everyone concerned will save time and money.

Mixing Is Time Domain; Mastering Is Frequency Domain

Time domain refers to tasks that happen "in time." For instance, the job of the mixing engineer is to choose the selection of best takes from those available and to get the balance right between all the tracks and all the various parts of the song—mixing the verse, then mixing the chorus and the bridge. These are time domain activities, which should be concerned not with the occasional frequency-based flaw of sibilance or boominess, but rather with how the file as a whole fits together as an individual song.

On the other hand, the mastering engineer is responsible for the *frequency domain*. This means, for example, compressing or limiting specific sibilant frequencies that should never be above a certain level, no matter at what time the sibilant event occurs within the file, and applying listening, learning, and logic to the file and the set of files to which it belongs. The desktop mastering plug-in chain is applied across the length of the entire track and applied in the frequency domain.

Time and frequency domain tasks are orthogonal (at right angles) to each other and are treated in the same way regardless of the ultimate format destination, be it for CD or digital distribution. That is why it is a good idea to separate the roles of mixing engineer and mastering engineer. The mastering engineer brings fresh ears and perspectives required to take the tracks to the finish line.

Sometimes, the mixing engineer won't like what the mastering engineer has done with the sound, but this can be a good thing. The best mixing engineers output premaster files that can have the very most made of them, and the files usually are not flashy in and of themselves. Those engineers' ears are tuned for a balanced, uncompressed sound, and this is what makes them good at their craft. The most important person in the equation is the client. If he or she is thrilled with the final output, the job has been appropriately completed. When the mixing engineer is the client, then we do what they say.

The Sound Pyramid: Artistic Rules

One issue I often see coming from inexperienced mixing engineers is unwieldy sound placement in the mix. There is a frequency and stereo placement structure to most pop, rock, and hip-hop music that should serve as a starting point based on the physical nature of the amplifier and speaker systems over which the music is reproduced. Once you understand why these basic guidelines are in place, feel free to play with them—but do so deliberately, not from ignorance.

Most importantly, keep your bass at the bottom. Low frequencies have very long wavelengths, which comes with a couple of implications. First, the frequencies are hard to localize—higher frequencies change rapidly enough to allow your hearing systems to zero in on where they originate. Lower frequencies, at the extreme, are more like barometric air-pressure changes: the whole room experiences higher and lower pressure as compared with the high frequencies that beam in straight lines from the speakers. Place your kick drums and (at least the low parts of) your bass guitar panned to center; these are generally mono and are a foundational part of the music, the base of the sound pyramid. This also allows both channels of the amplifier to share the work of reproducing these biggest of sounds.

Next, if the file is a vocal track, keep the vocal level and placement up front and center. Vocals are the top of the sound pyramid, the information carrier of the music. Having clear communication is vital and is one of the prime obligations we have as artists and as technical representatives for artists. The vocals can generally be panned to the center as well, since they won't interfere with the lower frequencies that also live in the center of the sound field. If the vocals are meant to function more as an instrument than a communicator, feel free to place them in any artistic space they call for. Likewise, if a lead instrument in an instrumental or a solo is taking the lead vocal's place, then that instrument or sound gets the lead vocal's spot—up front and center.

Layering frequency ranges is very important. Several instruments fighting for space in the mix will show up as mud—try to separate instruments with similar frequency ranges either through EQ (carve out a different primary range for each instrument) or stereo placement. Supporting instruments fill out the sides of the sound pyramid.

Three Functional Rules

The first most important mixing rule for premasters is to mix to 24-bit files rather than 16-bit files (a fully maxed 16-bit file, as seen in the first figure below, is equivalent to a 24-bit file turned down by 48 dB, as seen in the second figure). Even if you record at 16-bit, mix down to 24-bit for mastering. This should be provided as an option in the portion of your mixing application that covers rendering.

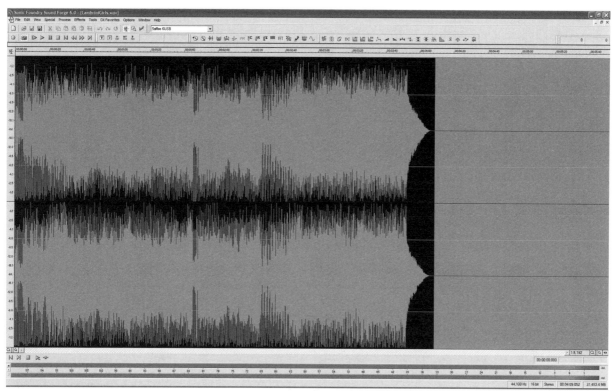

A Fully Maxed 16-bit File

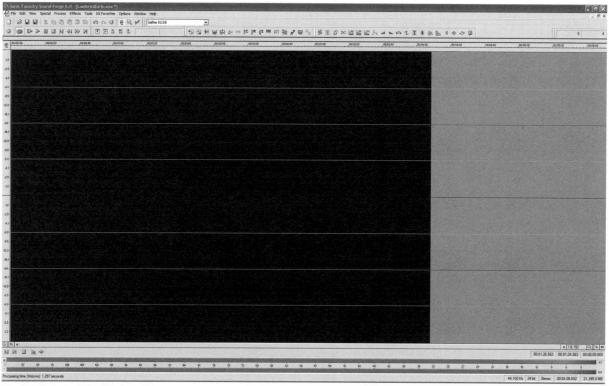

The Equivalent 16-bit File in 24-bit

Mixing to 24-bit allows you to implement the second most important mixing rule for premasters: leave 3 dB (or so) of headroom for the peaks, because the mastering engineer needs to be able to turn things up as well as turn things down. Even turning down a given frequency may "uninhibit" out-of-phase harmonics and result in a louder file, so the more headroom that's given the better. When a file comes in at 88.2 or 96 kHz/24-bit but is clipped and distorted, high sample rate and bit depth count for nothing. The file is damaged, and the mastering becomes a job of restoration.

The third, and equally important, rule for premasters is to avoid compression on the master bus. A good visual way to find out if you have too much compression is to look at the waveform of the mixed-down file in your workstation and note the top and bottom excursions. Do they look like a comb, as in the first figure below, or do they look straight, like a log, as in the second figure below? The flatter the tops and bottoms, the more compression and limiting have been applied. Even worse than compression at the premaster stage is limiting, which lessens the options mastering engineers have at their disposal to provide you with the best results possible.

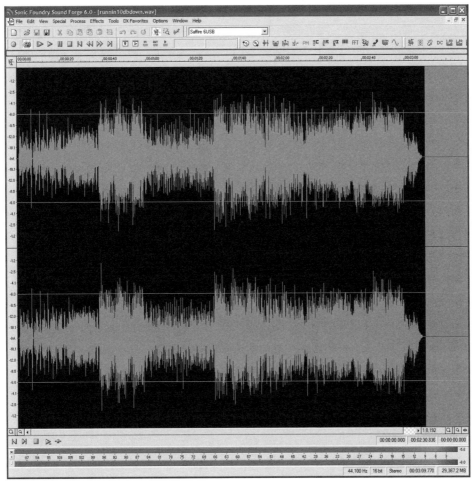

The Premaster as a Comb

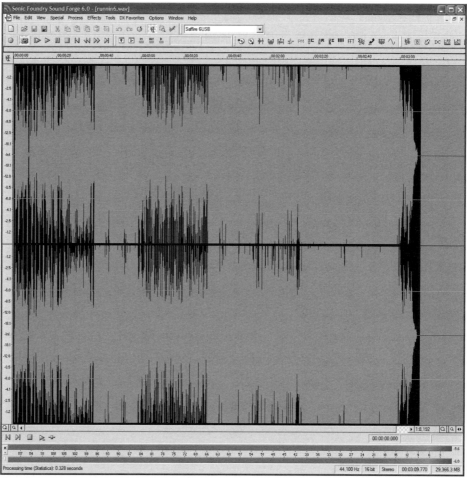

The Premaster as a Log

A good way of looking at this is to see the mastering engineer as an alchemist. It is his or her job to turn lead into gold. It is important when providing lead to an alchemist to provide pure lead, not fake gold.

Should You Include Start and End Fades in Mixing?

There are benefits to not having start and end fades in the premaster. The first good thing about leaving out fades is that some of the original noise in the recording situation may remain to capture an accurately modeled noiseprint within the noise reduction section of the mastering chain. There may be a noisy component in the background that comes up with the fade that could be easily addressed if there were a few seconds of studio sound isolating the problem sound or combinations of sounds at the beginning (or end) of the track.

This is well demonstrated in the first album I mastered, *Sticks and Stoned*, by Colour Twigs. We located the original tape, which started off with background tape noise, then guitar pedal noise, and then the beginning audio of the song. The section of the track that contained guitar pedal noise combined with background tape noise provided an excellent, accurate noiseprint source for the track, and made a great starting point for noise reduction.

The second, and more important, reason not to fade is that dynamic processing and various other processes in the mastering chain are often dependent on threshold and levels within the file. It is a delicate balance to set the levels such that they are optimized for the loudest sections of the track, but still have an acceptable effect during fades when the whole dynamic changes. This is most problematic with noise reduction settings (which is why my noise reduction thresholds are at the edge of audibility). If they are set too high, you'll hear the complement of the "keep residue" setting in the noise reduction plug-in, which can sound robotic and mechanical if not set correctly. So, leave at least a little room tone before and after the track to provide noiseprints, if necessary.

Horror Stories

Mysteries abound—I once received a track for a tribute album that looked like this:

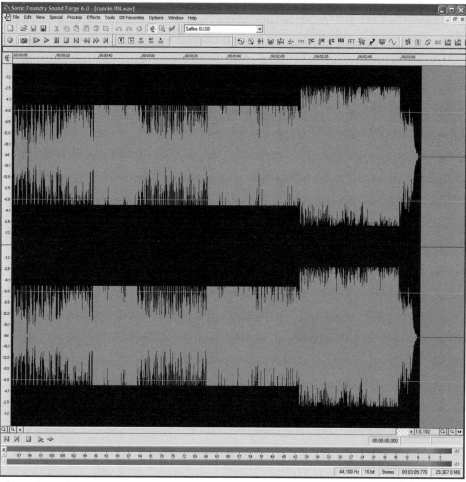

File as Originally Received

This was quite a head-scratcher—what could have happened to generate this track? It turned out that this was a collaborative track: the main music bed was done in New York, and sent to a guitarist in New Orleans to lay an outro guitar solo on. I found out later that the original track the guitarist received looked like this:

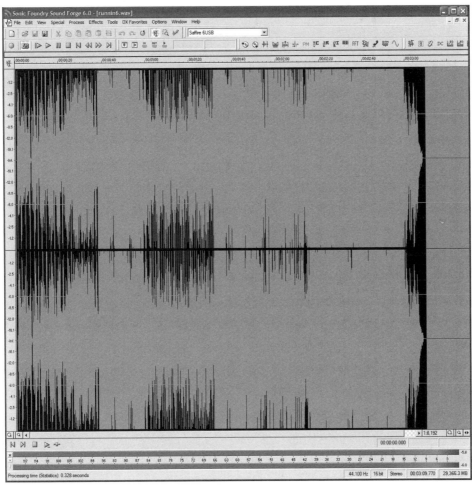

Music Bed Clipped

The next figure shows a closer look at the file:

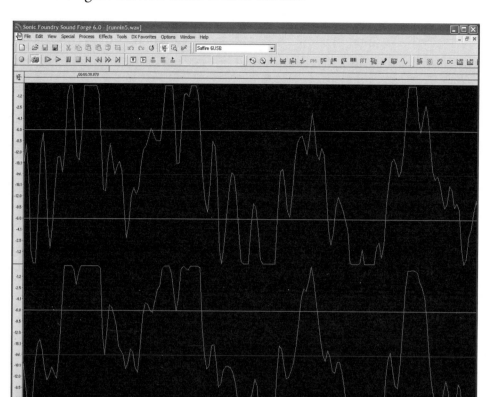

Music Bed Clipping Details

That's what the guitarist was sent to play his part on. So, he did the only thing he could do—reduce the whole file by 5 dB and lay his track down, which created the file I originally received. The guitarist's submission was pretty good—several decibels down (though still 16-bit, but these were earlier days when 24-bit was still computationally expensive).

What I received was a solid bar with the guitar solo coming up to full scale at the end of the song, with no explanation. I took a screen shot and sent it back to the original musician (who created the main music bed in New York) to ask if this was what he had in mind, and he replied that it had sounded good to him. I found this interesting, because the file looked really wrong.

After further investigation I figured out what was happening, but this entry would not be an acceptable premaster for our tribute album. I then asked both the original musician and the guitarist to send me their stem files (the separate files that make up the final track). I received the guitar part, and it looked great, as seen here:

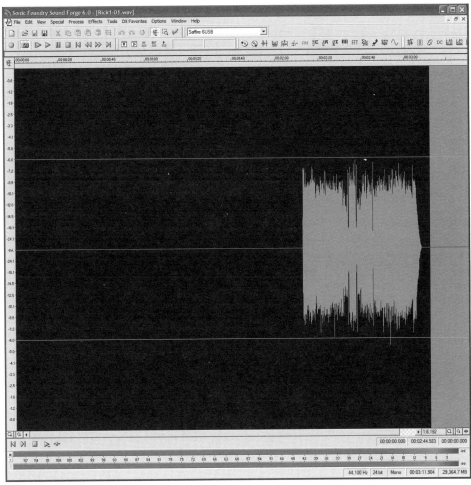

Guitar Solo Stem

The file I received from the original musician was the same clipped file that had been given to the guitarist, and was unworkable. I asked him to rerender the file 5 dB softer, and what you see in the next figure is what he sent, still quite clipped:

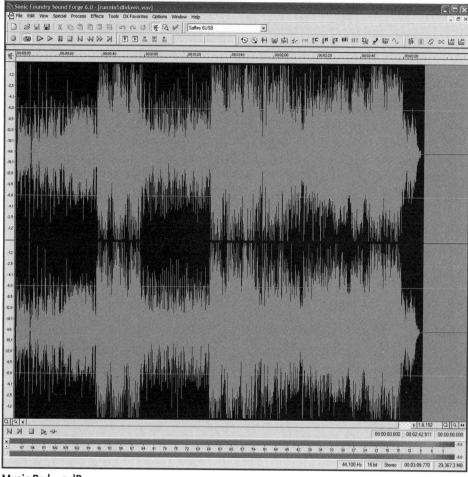

Music Bed, −5 dB

We tried again, this time asking him to drop the output by 10 dB and to please turn his compressor off. This resulted in the very workable file seen here:

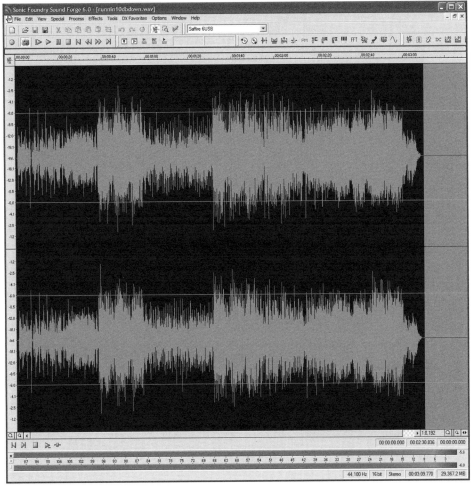

Music Bed, −10 dB

We took this file and the mono guitar solo over to producer and mixing engineer Steve Fisk to do some mixing magic with, and finally came up with the actual premaster for the file:

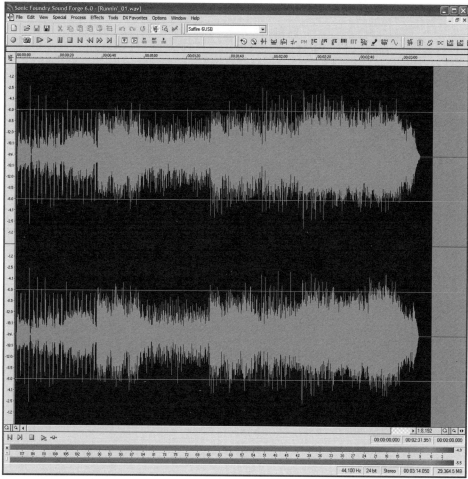

Fixed Mix Premaster File

This brings up the point that many audio people avoid looking at the waveform on the screen. Some insist that they just use their ears, and practically blindfold themselves when making audio decisions. I am of a different mind. I've learned a great deal about audio from watching the waveform go by. The dense, bright areas of high frequencies, the open spaces of low frequencies—these all inform me, like looking at a different dimension of the audio. The DVD-ROM accompanying this book contains videos of the sample files seen in this way.

In earlier days, I'd gauge from the brightness of the waveform as it sped by how sibilant the mastered file was. If it were "too bright" visibly, I'd go back and redo the file.

Multiple Versions

You'll typically want to render at least two versions of the mixes (especially if there are vocals). A full mix and an instrumental mix that are similar in every way besides the muted vocals are useful for licensing opportunities and for editing together censored versions of the tracks (splice in the instrumental portion during the censored words). This is also an opportunity to try to make a deal: if the instrumental and vocal files truly are equivalent enough to be processed by the same mastering chain, there is a good chance that your mastering engineer will master the instrumental version at no additional charge.

I have received several sets of files in which the instrumentals were way out of whack compared with the vocal versions, and I had to remaster each one. I threw these in for free, but really shouldn't have. Make sure that you look at the zoomed-out waveforms of your tracks before you send them off to be mastered.

Name Your Files Logically

Clear communication is one of the most important disciplines to work on with any service provider. The quality of the information you provide directly affects the results you receive in return. Send the artist name, song titles, song order—it is better to give too much information than too little. Also, try to keep the jargon down. I received a request from a young band after I sent them a mastered track for approval:

> Oh awesome! So this is the Song that is going to have a dog added to the end of it, like a bonus track, is it too late for this to be possible? :/ I feel bad that I didn't specify that the tracks are going to be connected. If it's a problem then let me know and we will try to figure it out. But thanks for every thing! They are sounding great :)

Needless to say, this was a bit confusing. A week later, as we were discussing the last track that needed mastering, I received this e-mail:

> Also, what our plan was was to have the song we're recording on Sunday to be on the same track as So Far So Good, and there be about 2 minutes of silence, kinda like a hidden track? So the album will look

like it'll only have 7 tracks, but the last track will have two songs! Also, Kyle meant "song", not "dog" haha.

This clarified things a bit—it turns out their producer used the slang "dog," as in "Let's get this dog finished," which is all well and good, but it made me scratch my head.

Alternatively, here is a message I received from a producer who knew what he was hearing and was able to clearly communicate his wishes to me (he wanted the new file to match a previously mastered file):

Hello Master Steve,

After listening back 4 or 5 times and referencing Frustration (the previous file), I would like one more pass thru to treat the following:

I think the track will complement the tones of Frustration if we slightly reduce some Upper-mids to reduce a little bite from the guitars as well as the Highs present in the cymbals.

The Low end could use a little fullness supporting the bass guitar; the tune is centered in B so look at Octaves 3-5... You know your signal chain the best and the octaves reference is just a guide.

The volume levels of both tracks sounded fairly even so no change there, but there's dynamic limiting... please add a slight tweak to the limiting with the intention to balance (not squash) the mix and again complement the dynamics of Frustration. With Frustration I remember addressing the width of the stereo field?

Please e-mail the link to new files to both [*XXX*] and myself, as we are on a tight schedule for CD duplication; I will send $$ via PayPal tomorrow night.

Thanks again for your support.

[*Producer name*]

Phone: (XXX) XXX-XXXX

He gives plenty of information, and the critical human factors: his phone number, and a promise of payment. We like to see these messages from clients.

Another surprising communication issue came up while mastering a band with quite a lot of experience. They were producers and "rock stars" in their own right, but they made a rookie mistake when they sent me their songs. Each song was titled with a number, 1 to 7. Then in one of a flurry of e-mails, they mentioned the track order being 5, 2, 4, 6, 1, 3 7. This didn't make sense to me, and I delivered the album by the track number order, 1 to 7. On listening to the disc, the client called up and said that the tracks were all out of order. It turned out that they had named the tracks in the order they had composed them, and grew accustomed to those single-digit names. This generated more trouble than benefit in the long run. I did resequence the disc, and it turned out to be pretty popular. This same disc was slated to be pressed to vinyl (which I do not do), but it turned out that the masters I made for the CD and digital release were workable on a record lathe as well, which was reassuring.

Even worse was the client who used an Alesis Masterlink to mix down to, which by default names each track Song 01, Song 02, and so on. I received several different files all with these same names (and with 88.2 kHz sample rates—huge files that I immediately converted to 44.1 kHz). Challenging.

Do Things in the Right Order

The same client that sent the huge files all named the same managed to keep making a lot of work for me over the course of the project (without further compensation). The first of those 88.2 kHz files was fully clipped along the entirety of the song.

This was for a brand-new client that lived out of state, who came to record with an engineer in town that I hadn't worked with before, so I was excited to make a good first impression. I made it clear that the best process flow started with receiving the very first file that had been mixed, therefore having a chance to comment before the rest of the tracks were mixed—especially on a first-contact situation.

Well, the file came in—and this was to be my first demo for the artist to ensure the project. The following e-mail conversation ensued:

Hi [*Artist name*],

This is why it is a good idea to do one song first… Is it possible to get this track rerendered with the peaks 2 to 3 dB down? It is very hot for a premaster.

If it is not possible, I can go ahead with this version. Ideally, let's get a rerender. Let me know.

Thanks!

…Steve>>>

Hi Steve,

I'm not sure what rerender means.

But I will have [*Engineer name*] rerender the file.

Thanks for letting me know.

In the meantime, would you like another file to work with?

[*Artist name*]

Dear [*Artist name*],

Sure, send another song. Rerender just means mix down to stereo (render) the full mix, but turn the outputs down a bit while doing so. [*Engineer name*] should know what I mean—feel free to have him get in touch with me if desired, as well.

Thanks!

…Steve>>>

Hey Steve,

[*Engineer name*] said it's fine. He's not willing to rerender any of the songs we've done so far, and we've done six songs, so the versions you'll be receiving from me are the mixes for mastering. I'm not sure if the final or mastered product will be affected greatly, with what I'm now told have peaks in the masterlink playback? But please go ahead with a demo master for me :-) please feel free to give me a call on my cell if you have any questions or concerns at XXX-XXX-XXXX. You can also give [*Engineer name*] a call as he is more knowledgeable in this subject than I am. His number is XXX-XXX-XXXX.

Thanks,

[*Artist name*]

So, I was stuck to try to make this fully clipped file work. Fortunately, it was a 24-bit file, so I could turn the level down without fear of resolution loss. I gave it a go, returning it to the artist and engineer (who by this time were mostly through with mixing the album). The feedback I received on that first demo was that it was too compressed. This came during my first phone conversation with the engineer. I explained about gain structure and that there was actually distortion in the file, but he replied that he doesn't worry about the small things—it's the music that is important. I sighed, and offered to try again with this first demo mastering. We agreed on that, and that he would get back to me with his comments, which read as follows:

Hi Steve,

Much Better on Vers 2. Just be careful not to crush the cymbals down too much.

I still want to hear the crashes punch through without getting flattened like a pancake.

I think overall loudness should be secondary to good tone and instrument mix relationships.

Of course it needs to be louder than the mix is.

It has a nice clear sound on initial listening. I'm hearing a nice freq balance, perhaps a teensy bit bright.

Overall stereo imaging-good!

Nice job!

Thanks,

[*Engineer name*]

Did you notice what killed me? The engineer is asking it to be louder than the mix is, on a fully clipped file. Challenging. Another issue with this project was that my responses and turnarounds were always within one day, and the responses from the artist and engineer usually took several days to arrive. I had quoted that this album should take about two days to complete, and if things had occurred in the correct order, that would have been an easy target to accomplish.

The artist then sent a message asking if I had received any comments from the engineer (which weren't copied to the artist) and requesting my take on the mixed files. I forwarded the above comments with my response:

Hi [*Artist name*]!

Glad to hear from you! Attached are the notes from [*Engineer name*] regarding the second try.

My notes on the delivered mix are the same as they have been from the beginning; an appropriate premaster should be 2 to 3 dB down from full scale and not be clipping across the entire file. There is also audible distortion in the file.

[*Engineer name*] and I had a discussion on the phone on Thursday where I told him exactly the tools I use in mastering, and the importance of appropriate gain structure and staging. He asked me to give it another try with less compression (which is fine, there are several styles we master for). Version 3 is the one with the least compression. In [*Engineer name*]'s note below, he directs that the mastered track be louder than the mix—but when the mix is already clipping, that could be problematic.

Feel free to call if you wish—I have been concerned by the lack of response to this so far. I understand that we are still in mastering demo land, and I've been looking forward to a second track (that is an appropriate premaster) to demonstrate my mastering style.

With warmest regards,

…Steve>>>

This led to weeks of uploading issues for the artist (since the files were so big) and several more challenging files. The engineer finally put up the files in his workstation, and the next time we talked, he apologized for the state of the files, now seeing what he had actually sent me. To his credit, this resulted in a series of very good tracks coming out of the studio, and the last two were sent at 44.1 kHz (my preferred rate), so we were making good progress.

After completing the mastering, I typically have the artist approve each track that I send them (both in .wav and MP3), and arrange a calendar event for CD sequencing, during which they tell me what song order and spacing they want their finished disc to have. This is the next conversation that happened after delivering the final two tracks to the artist:

hi steve,

thanks so much for these.

any chance you and send a reference cd to [*Engineer name*]?

he's asking for one so he can listen to them back to back without clicking on each link, as well as being able to play them in other stereo systems more conveniently.

not sure if that's an odd request. but if you're able to do that for him, that would be greatly appreciated.

i'm wondering if i need one too. is the mp3 the same quality as the wav file? it's not right?

would you mind sending me a reference cd as well?

let me know. thanks!

[*Artist name*]

K, please send me your CD song order (and their full titles), thanks!

…Steve>>>

A while later, the actual track names and the sequence order of the tracks arrived. Usually, the artist or engineer comes to the studio to sequence to ensure song spacing is to their liking. I am happy to sequence on my own, knowing I'll be sending a full-length reference .wav file and MP3 to the artist for their approval on the sequencing order and spacing, along with a full track cue sheet including ISRC codes (more on those in a later chapter). After that process is approved, I'll go ahead and make a Production Master CD and a listening copy for the artist, and we're done.

Accordingly, I sequenced the tracks and generated the reference CD files for approval, and sent them along with this note:

Hi [*Artist name*],

Here is the track list and ISRC codes for the CD. I went ahead and sequenced the disc, and will upload the full disc in wav and mp3 for your approval (especially on track spacing).

Thanks!

…Steve>>>

And in response:

Steve,

[*Engineer name*] is asking for an actual CD.

He doesn't want to listen to it online.

He wants to be able to take it to his car

And put it in other peoples stereo system.

Would you mind giving him a CD?

Also any chance you can do the same for me?

Thanks :-)

One missing item here are addresses to send these CDs to, which the artist sent after my request. Usually, the normal process is to approve the sequence, then get the CDs. The project had been backwards from the start. So, with limited information, I offered and delivered two complete sets of Production Master CDs and listening copies to the artist and engineer. I mailed the set to the artist, and hand-delivered the set to the engineer.

Several days later I received the following e-mail:

Hi Steve,

I got a chance to listen to the cd you sent me. [*Engineer name*] also listened to it and made some comments. I think it's great. Awesome job on mastering. The things we've noticed that will need changing is that the transition between songs should be at least another 0.5 seconds. Also, the text should read [*Full artist name*] and not just [*Artist name*]. [*Engineer name*] mentioned that "[*Song name*]" may need to have more dynamics. When I listened to the cd in the car, I noticed that I had to turn the volume all the way up to the 30s in order to hear it. It could be my car speakers, but I'm not sure. Those are my thoughts.

Do you mind making those changes as far as text and transition time? Please ask [*Engineer name*] about "[*Song name*]" and dynamics. If you get a chance to pop the Cd in your car, let me know what level volume you're on to hear it clearly and comfortable.

Thanks :-)

[*Artist name*]

The lesson to take away from this situation (still in progress) is to please make sure that you are familiar with the process chain that your mastering engineer has, and do your best to provide complete project information in the right order for a timely conclusion to projects.

File-Name Conventions

My preferred incoming-file naming convention is Artist_Name-Track_Name_DDMMMYY.wav. For an additional benefit append the CD track order number (if you know it) to the beginning of the file name, and always include a file-name extension—PCs, at least, require them. No need to have your service provider guessing about file types.

Preflight Checklist

When your mix is complete and ready to go, there are several questions to ask about the track. Many of these should have been taken care of at tracking time, but just to make sure:

- Is it in time?
- Is it in tune?
- Is it in tone?
- Is the balance correct?
- Is the level correct?
- Is the phase correct?
- Is the resolution correct?

Premaster Transport

At the time of this writing I take tracks via YouSendIt (yousendit.com), Dropbox (dropbox.com), or SoundCloud (soundcloud.com). Getting files this way brings 24-bit/44.1 kHz files into my studio immediately from the client. Sometimes I get premasters on audio CDs (which are 16-bit), but I highly prefer 24-bit files.

YouSendIt

Functional description: A one-way Internet file-transmission service, used to receive and send large files.

I have an annual subscription and an Internet drop box with YouSendIt, which serves me excellently as a file-transfer method. The branded drop box lets potential clients know exactly my preferred file preferences and provides a simple interface to send me their data files (up to 2 GB in size). When files are uploaded to my drop box, I am notified via e-mail, and

Ars Divina YouSendIt Dropbox

run the very convenient YouSendIt express application that takes care of downloads in the background and restarts on errors without user intervention. After I master the track (or tracks), I generate an MP3 file and send it and the mastered track back to the client, also via YouSendIt. They get a notification over e-mail, and download the files. If it is a single-file job, end of story. Otherwise, the client is updated file by file throughout the duration of the project.

Dropbox

Functional description: A shared folder on the computer desktop, shared with an arbitrary number of people.

Dropbox.com

Dropbox is very handy for large projects that go through many changes from many people (for instance, our Burning Sky Records record label is a big user of Dropbox). At times, bands will share their drop boxes with me to access their premasters, and request that I return the masters in a separate "mastered" drop-box directory. At this point, up to a 2 GB drop box is provided at no charge, but can be limiting if you have several clients using them. Dropbox has a 50 and 100 GB offering for annual fees. I went with the 50 GB option right away—I can service up to 25 clients, each provided with a complementary 2 GB drop box.

This is not my preferred method of premaster file access, however. Once I master a track (or set of tracks), I'm just as happy to archive the tracks and not have them in active storage on my desktop. The one-way transient nature of YouSendIt is preferred, for my purposes.

SoundCloud

Functional description: YouTube for .wav files

SoundCloud

In addition to being a great collaboration and production tool (SoundCloud allows private workspaces with timed comments on high-resolution files, as in the figure below), SoundCloud offers a branded drop-box service at a higher-premium level and provides 128 kbps MP3 streaming in widgets. The service provides shortcuts for sharing to social-media networks, so that I can embed a .wav image with a play button on Facebook or any website that allows comments. Each track also has options for metadata: images, bpm, and links to where a version of the file can be bought.

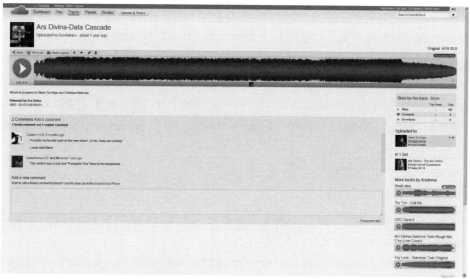

A SoundCloud Track with a Timed Comment

SoundCloud also allows those who play the track to share it virally as well, in e-mail and on social sites, quite friction free (easy to do). Another share method for SoundCloud files is an HTML string that beautifully embeds in HTML-aware comments fields. This provides a strategy to post your tracks to your favorite artist's data cascades, and their other viewers may have a higher likelihood of enjoying it. The track can also be flagged to be downloadable as a full lossless .wav file, which is a real benefit if you want the full quality of your work to be appreciated. Personally, I think the very idea of data transfer even needing to be mentioned as an issue will be quaint soon.

5

The Mastering Process

In the mastering process, as in life, we begin at the beginning. Once you have arranged the business aspects of the relationship with your clients, be they producer or artist, it's time to receive the file.

Receiving the Premaster

The premastered file(s) can come in digitally or physically on CD or data disc, but ideally at the end of receiving them you have a stereo .wav file that you'll need to put somewhere in order to work on it. I have a download directory that I back up regularly and an additional drive with an audio directory, within which are separate subdirectories named for each client.

If this is a new client, go to your audio directory and create an artist-name directory and copy the premaster file to this directory. It is a good idea to keep the original file intact in your download directory and work on the copy—you never know when you'll need a backup.

Also, create a subdirectory named Complete in each artist directory. This is where you'll put each mastered file and the finished files for production.

Prepare for Mastering

Start up your mastering software and load all the tracks for the job into your workstation. It is a good idea to "tile" their windows and zoom each file out within its individual window so you can see at a glance what you have to work with; for example, are the files consistent in level, or all over the map? Note their bit depth—are they 24-bit or better? This is a good time to learn to fail fast, meaning that if the files have problems, go back to the client and see if he or she can provide more suitable files.

A good time to save the workspace for the job in your program is when the files are initially up and tiled. This provides the benefit that if you are called away to another job, you can come back and recall all the files at once. Another good habit to get into is to tile and save the file workspace at the end of each session, with just the remaining files to work on—this makes for a quick startup when you get back to the job.

Check that all the files sample rates are set to 44.1 kHz (resample if necessary). Since the end result of your plug-in chain is 44.1 kHz (and there is no opportunity to change the sample rate within the plug-in chain), it is important to begin with the final desired sample rate.

The Start Noise

Next, for each file, add two seconds of start noise. This is a solution that came about from needing to resolve a problem with the C4 Parametric Processor stage of the chain (which we'll explore in detail later). This trick proved to have utility across the whole plug-in chain, and provides an informational touchstone as well.

The C4, like any complicated tool, is not without its quirks and unique methods of operation. In the C4's case, there was an issue that I found out about during an audition to master an entire license library of music—around 3,000 tracks. The file I was sent to work on had a very long and slow attack. Going through my standard mastering chain, this attack slowly came up to the threshold of the C4 and demonstrated a "feature anomaly." When the levels in each band were sufficiently low, the EQ curve "drooped" very audibly in the low-level bands. And as the attack increased up to the thresholds, the EQ "snapped" into place—also very audibly. This was a career crisis for me—3,000 tracks lay in the balance. You can see the "droop" in the figure below and in the C4 time-lapse image in the figure following.

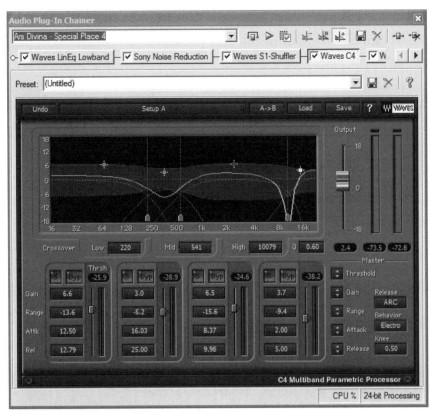

Waves C4 Prethreshold Droop

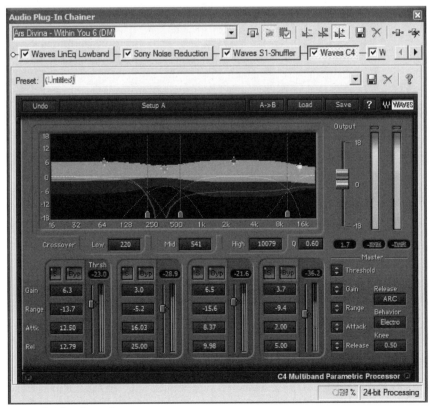

Waves C4 Time-lapse Image

I called the folks at Waves tech support. They hadn't been aware of the issue, but recommended adding some signal before the file to snap past the thresholds.

I finally settled on adding two seconds of noise at the beginning of every file, which has a couple of great unintended benefits. The initial functionality of the starting noise is to energize the entire plug-in chain to get all the plug-ins over their thresholds, avoiding the lurching start that slow attacks and, to a lesser extent, any soft sounds in the beginning of tracks, cause. The unintended benefit is that within two seconds, by listening to the noise I can tell everything this particular plug-in chain preset is doing. Is the track louder? Softer? Brighter? Dimmer? I can tell, because the source noise is the same every time. This has been a *great* benefit to my work.

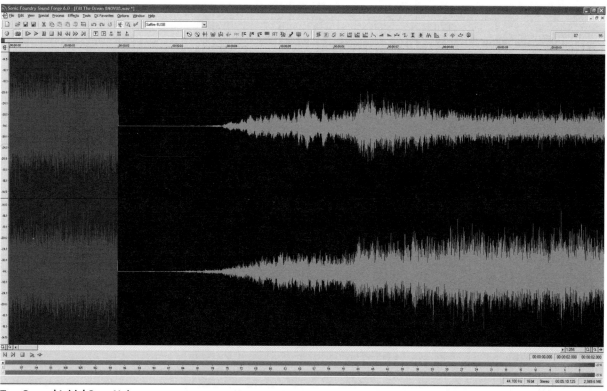

Two-Second Initial Start Noise

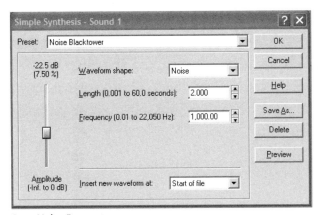

Start Noise Parameters

Finally, save each file to the artist directory.

Generate a Default Plug-in Chain for the Project

When mastering a whole CD project for a client, the first step (of course) is to master the first track. The saved plug-in chain for that track typically will be the default for the rest of the files in the project, assuming that the project is reasonably similar song to song and is made by the same engineers in the same studio over a reasonably short time. Sometimes, the tracks vary quite a bit from song to song, especially if they were done at different times and at different studios. You'll still want to have a standard baseline plug-in chain for the project—I consider that to be the "trunk of the tree." It's the first place to start from on the next track.

Some types of music, especially hip-hop, have multiple versions of tracks to be mastered:

1. The uncensored vocal version
2. The "clean" (censored) version
3. The show version
4. The instrumental version

It is a good idea to master these tracks in this order as well. The uncensored vocal version has everything there is in the track. The settings in the plug-in chain for this version transfer well for the other tracks—as opposed to beginning with the instrumental without the sibilance of the lead vocal, which is needed to tune the chain for reuse as a preset for the next version.

The clean version has most of what the full version has, and if there is a stereo issue (as there often is), it typically occurs in the vocals—so the full-version setting should work fine for the clean version. The show version has backing vocals on it, but no lead vocal. This is used at shows as backing tracks, hence the name. The (hip-hop) show version probably wants enhanced bass for bigger impact over P.A. speakers.

6

The Desktop Mastering Chain

I've had to learn a lot in the years of refining the desktop mastering plug-in chain, and that admission can be a challenge to the ego. When I go back and look at the chains that predated my current standards, I see items that make me cringe a little bit. For instance, in the early days of using the LinEQ Lowband, I would have the dither set to "on" (its default setting), and have the unused filter sections selected. The early dithering issue was pointed out to me during an Audio Engineering Society meeting where I was giving a mastering chain demonstration—and the point was very valid. On my next job, I turned off the dither and the unused bands, and the sound noticeably (but subtly) cleared up.

This led to a great lesson: learn to fail fast, always keep an open mind about your processes, and try not to grow too attached to them. Realize that your future self has different standards, and constantly seek out what they will be.

Get Them While They're Young: The Waves LinEQ Lowband

The Waves LinEQ Lowband is the first stage of the chain. As a rule, there is a highpass filter at 20 Hz to remove DC offset. The other action at this stage is to provide rough control

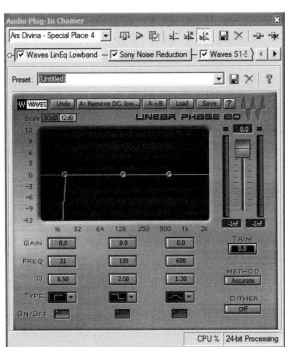

The Waves LinEQ Lowband

over the low end. Here is where you carve (or, very rarely, boost) the low end. It is also where you attenuate overly loud premasters. Let's begin with one of the most critical aspects of a functional chain: gain structure, or the level that each plug-in presents to the next plug-in in line.

Each plug-in in the desktop mastering chain is in its proper functional order. The LinEQ Low Band is at the beginning and cuts off what is not needed. This is the stage at which overall level can be tamed if the submitted file is too loud (something that happens all too often). It is also the place where you can attack the strongest unwanted levels, the bass frequencies.

Counterintuitively, having less bass allows for a larger sound. Most project studios do not have adequate low-frequency monitoring systems, so tracks are mixed with the low end that "sounds right." In reality, however, there may be *way* too much bass in the signal, which effectively reduces headroom and squishes the high end riding on those bass cycles right into the ceiling. The solution in many cases is to turn the bass down right at the start of the chain.

Alternatively, if a file is weak in bass, this is the first stage at which you can boost it. It is important to understand the interactions between the processors in the plug-in chain: the bass you modify here has a strong interaction with the bass section of the Waves C4 Parametric Processor a few stages down the line.

The three filter sections provided by the LinEQ Lowband are switchable between five different filter types. For our purposes you need only two of them: the digital highpass and the digital low shelf.

The first filter is always set as a digital highpass, set at 21 Hz, with the method type set to Accurate and the Q set to the steepest, 6.5, which gives a near-brickwall filter slope. If

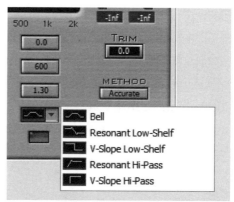

LinEQ Lowband Filter Types

there are no significant issues with low end in the mix, this takes care of the DC offset in the file, and you're done with this stage.

DC Offset Explained

DC offset is a pesky, subtle issue that is solved by using the highpass 20 Hz brickwall filter right at the beginning of your processing. DC (which stands for "direct current," as compared to "AC," or "alternating current") is zero cycles per second, which is lower than 20 Hz. Standard waveforms are usually AC, alternating above and below the zero amplitude line (which is the speaker at rest).

DC is a lack of up-and-down motion, and DC offset is the shifting of the zero point of the waveform up or down. One source of DC offset can be from miscalibrated analog-to-digital converters, which send out positive or negative numbers when the input is at rest (and should be generating all zeros), or from unbalanced differential amplifiers. Sometimes it's just a mystery where DC offset and other audio artifacts originate.

A key in mastering is to adjust everything toward a relaxed, unstrained position. DC offset results in the speakers not cycling evenly through zero. There is an analog to this that we have all experienced—in elevators. When you go up in an elevator and your ears need to pop, that is DC offset. It is the pressure behind your eardrums being out of balance with the air pressure in the room. Just as this is uncomfortable to experience, it also provides a strain on the speakers and audio content. A remarkable example of DC offset can be seen in the following:

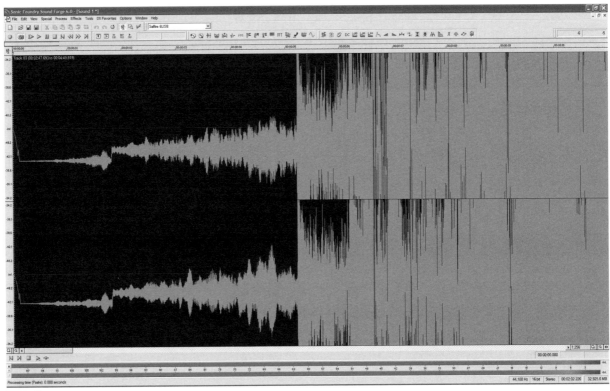

DC Offset

Zero Hz is lower than 20 Hz, and the LinEQ Lowband is set as a brickwall, highpass filter at 20 Hz. A highpass filter allows only higher frequencies to pass into the audio chain (hence the name highpass)—any lower frequencies are blocked. And since DC offset has a frequency of zero (it never crosses the center line), this filter blocks all DC offset problems, regardless of whether they are offset high or low.

It is interesting to notice in this case that we are taking what appears to be a time domain problem (the DC offset, which potentially happens throughout the entire file with potentially different values at different times in the file) and applying a frequency domain solution, by looking at DC offset as a zero amplitude frequency event. Therefore, instead of selecting and offsetting every errant section, we run the highpass filter just once for the entire file. This is a good problem-solving lesson—to approach problems from different directions.

In the early days of desktop mastering, before the plug-in chain, each of these processors in the chain was run *serially*, or one at a time. The way I used to adjust for DC offset was to run the statistics of the file, which provided a readout of the values of DC offset in each channel. Then, I'd pull up the DC Offset tool (which allows moving the file up and down around the zero line) and enter the opposite (complementary) values in the tool. For instance, if the statistics gave a value of "9" for DC Offset, I would correct by moving the entire file down by "–9".

This was problematic, since most files did not have just a single DC offset issue. If there were included samples or recorded tracks with variable DC offset values, this method would just average them all out but not solve the underlying problem. Hence, the LinEQ Lowband solution in the frequency domain: the 20 Hz highpass filter locks the entire file around the zero point, regardless of the direction or quantity of the DC offset.

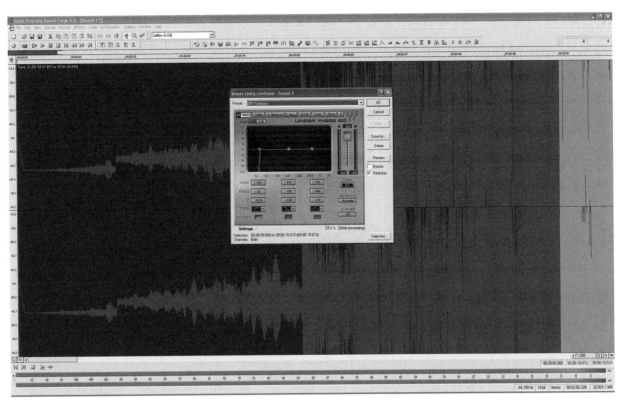

Before LinEQ Lowband

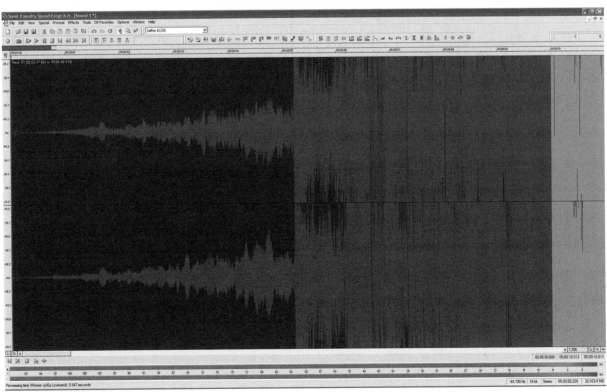

After LinEQ Lowband

Back to Setting the LinEQ Low Band

If there is too much (or too little) low end in the file, go to the second filter (since the first one is your brickwall at 20 Hz) and select the digital low-shelf filter type. At this point, often with a cutoff frequency starting at around 100 to 140 Hz and a moderate Q of 2.5, raise or lower the filter until the bass sounds appropriately balanced with the rest of the frequency ranges. Make this judgment based on the full plug-in chain—not with this or other individual bands and plug-ins soloed. The mixes that need this kind of attention usually originate from studios without appropriately calibrated subwoofers. Most people want to hear the low end and will boost the very low end for it to show up at all in their monitors.

If that still doesn't do the trick, or if there are several low-end problems, you may have to engage the third filter, also set as a digital low shelf. The cutoff for this filter may be as high as 250 Hz. Here is where we come into another basic concept of desktop mastering, called *leverage*. When you adjust the third filter, it is not in isolation—you are also affecting the second filter levels. Any move on any filter may (and often does) require a balancing move on another affected filter. So, if you find it necessary to cut a lot at the third filter, remember to bring the second filter up a bit and average out the move—find beauty in balance.

Keep Them Quiet: Noise Reduction

Noise reduction algorithms use a *noiseprint*, a clean sample of the sound that you want to detect and remove (*buzz, hiss, hum,* and so on). If the beginning of a tune hasn't been trimmed, this noise is usually present before the instruments come in. The noiseprint can be relatively long or short (typically short), depending on what it takes to capture the offending sound. Highlight the selection you've chosen for the noiseprint, and play it back in looped mode; the sound should be smooth and regular, with no significant discontinuities such as clicks or pops.

How Noise Reduction Algorithms Work

The program translates the noiseprint into a series of noise-gate threshold points (creating a noiseprint envelope) shown in graphical form. Each point represents a particular narrow frequency band (there can be thousands of bands in a noiseprint).

Signals lower than each point's height (threshold level) are considered as noise. When the noise reduction plug-in is active, the program monitors playback for any frequencies that fit this profile that are quieter than or equal to these levels. If they are found, the corresponding bands are reduced in level; in other words, the gate goes from "on" or "open" to a lower volume level set by the "Reduce noise by (dB)" setting, but not necessarily gated fully off. This is the process that removes the noise. Typical attenuation amounts are 15 to 20 dB, although the optimum amount varies depending on the application. My default reduction is 20 dB; special-purpose settings can be more extreme.

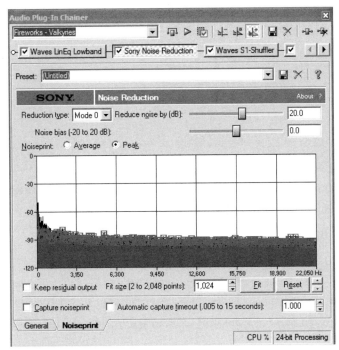

Sony Noise Reduction

The bumpy line in figure above is composed of little boxes, each of which is the threshold of a noise gate at a specific frequency. In this case, there are 1,024 noise gates across the frequency spectrum. So, if you have bass notes soloing in your track without content in the high end, hiss in the high end (that you don't want) is gated. For instance, there is a common noise spike in many noiseprints at 15 kHz, a flyback frequency from Mac computer monitors, as seen in following figure.

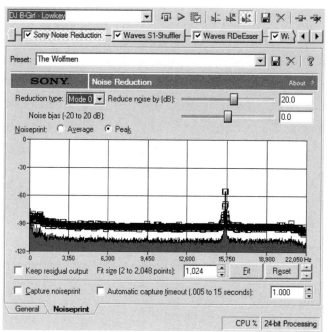

15 kHz Mac Monitor Flyback

Our theme in these early stages of the chain is "get them when they're young"—the idea is to take care of a lot of very subtle details before you *take gain* (turn up the volume). If you're going to take the noise out, take it out when the file is still somewhat soft and quiet. If you take gain first, then you are just working against yourself.

Noise Reduction Threshold Setting

Although noise may seem audible only during quiet passages and breaks, remember that it's always in the background and subtly masking the over-all sound, and the ability to properly set the noise gate thresholds is part of the craft of mastering.

A noise gate in this case has two main parameters: threshold and reduc-tion level. Each of the 1,024 noise gates across the frequency range has its threshold set either by a noiseprint (which measures the level of the noiseprint sample at each gate frequency position and sets the threshold at that level) or by being manually placed and moved. Typically, you'll want to have control and modify and fine-tune the levels of your sampled noiseprint.

When I started learning how to use the noise reduction plug-in, I would try to find a noiseprint for every track I worked on. Finding a noise sample is tough sometimes if the mixing engineer does not anticipate what the mastering engineer needs. Not providing preroll and postroll on the file (in other words, cutting right at the beginning and end) removes an opportunity to find a good noise source. If the mixing engineer gates all the tracks, then the noise to be removed is always masked by the signal. Sometimes, there are pauses in the music that can expose a good noise sample. Ideally, the files you get in to master have some room tone or the sound of the mixing console isolated before the song itself starts.

One of the places where noise reduction shines is in audio restoration—occasionally for legal forensics and 911 calls, but typically from records and tapes. The archiving of these media is a luxury, because the beginnings of the tracks typically present record or tape noise; and when the record button is engaged yet another noise-scape presents itself. It is at that combined stage where you ideally want to take the noiseprint sample from.

For instance, in the first Colour Twigs album mastering I did, we eventually did get the original reel-to-reel premaster tapes digitized. At the beginning of the tracks, there was the tape noise. Then, fortunately, there was a second or two of "all foot pedals, mics, and synthesizers on" noise. This provided an ideal selection area to take a noiseprint, and the resulting audio was cleaner than even the sound in the studio when the track was recorded! Gordon Raphael (the vocalist) was shocked to hear his bracelet rattle near the mic before one song, which he had never heard in the earlier versions.

Tuning the Noiseprint

Once you get a workable noiseprint from an appropriate selection, I recommend editing the individual noise gates in the very lowest end of the frequency range: 200 Hz and below. Thresholds set using a noiseprint typically have quite a bit of extra low-frequency energy in the noise sample, which shows up as a rising slope to the left in the noiseprint. If kept that way, the results are typically detectable and the low-end quality of the track suffers—so I regularly flatten out that rising leftward slope to match the average threshold levels across the frequency range (that is a quality desktop mastering secret).

After you have modified the noiseprint to be relatively flat, select all the threshold points and check the Keep Residual Output box. Play the file, and listen to the scritchy sounds coming out. Next, slowly lift all the selected thresholds up until the output sounds like the full-range audio, and then slowly pull the line of threshold boxes down until you are just hearing noise without too much music content. As you listen to the residual noise, you'll hear a robotic, machinelike grinding sound at some point between the full audio and the quiet noise settings. It is important to understand that the complement of this sound is heard in the music (which is one way to detect and hear a poorly calibrated noise reduction stage). In general, the noise reduction is set correctly when there is minimal tonal content in the residue.

This noise gate threshold level is a variable setting depending on the incoming audio. Sometimes you want to carve out a bunch of low-level distortion that is getting in the way of clarity further down the chain— I've worked with noisy punk bands that benefited quite a lot from harsh hash reduction. In the greatest number of cases, the threshold setting will generally be around –90 dB or lower, almost imperceptible.

These days, I have taken to having a standard noiseprint start setting. If more tuning is necessary for the particular track, I'll seek out an appropriate noiseprint. Otherwise, I'll set the threshold level as described above, and that typically takes care of this stage of the chain.

The practical function of the noise reduction plug-in is to provide a dynamic-range enhancement. Later on in the chain when we take gain, the low-level noise that was at –90 dB doesn't become a much more audible –70 dB; since we are dropping the noise floor by 20 dB, we have that much more headroom. In this case, the gain can be increased by 20 dB later on down the chain, and the noise floor will be perceived as having the same level as the premastered track.

The Reversal Trick: Reverse Noise Reduction

At the beginning of my desktop mastering career in 1997, computers were very slow in manipulating the "large" file sizes of digital audio, compared with current standards. Each stage in the plug-in chain had to be run separately and serially, one after another. It took more than ten minutes just to run each stage, and if you cut any audio from the beginning of a track and saved the track, the file had to be fully rewritten to disc, which was also a several-minute exercise. Deleting sections at the end of the file did not have that penalty and saved right away.

The early evolution of the desktop mastering process was to listen through each song until something popped out and irritated you as a listener, and then to solve that issue and go to the next. As soon as the file was completely neutralized, with no irritating features, it was usually ready to go into the Waves Ultramaximizer and be complete. This was a rather long and tedious process, typically taking around four hours to master a single four-minute song. There were benefits to this, however: the engineer was able to get a really good intuitive grasp of exactly what each processor was doing to the sound, and how the track sounded "in between processes"—something that we don't really have now.

Another benefit of serial plug-in chaining was non-real-time processing. For instance, I discovered a valuable trick that I can no longer use now that we have the chain. At the noise reduction stage I would reverse the file, run the noise reduction, and then reverse the file again. The benefit of this is that most impulses in music have a fast attack and slow release. However, subtle noise gates don't like to open abruptly—they're much happier tracking a relatively slow curve.

When the noise reduction parameters were set up and the file reversed, the impulses had a slow attack and quick release, which made the gates much happier. This worked because noise is the same going forward or backward. So if you turn the file backward during noise reduction, you are actually opening up on the releases and falling off on the attacks. When you reverse the file back again to play forward, it's as if the noise gates are predictive—when a sharp attack comes up in the track, the noise gate opens just prior to its arrival.

After the noise reduction was applied, and I had reversed the file to continue hunting anomalies, a workflow process presented itself. While the file was reversed, I'd cut off what was then the tail of the song, which became the top of the song during normal play. This got me around the file-saving time penalty of deleting time from the beginning of the track.

Another benefit of this process was that I heard a lot of backwards audio. For instance, there was a gospel choir with a soloist who had an incredibly round tone to her voice; her attacks and releases were very similar. Played backwards, her voice sounded like an angelic alien, and I was able to use the backwards sample in a different track.

Special Purposes Fixes

The figure below shows an example of using the noise reduction plug-in as a notch filter. In an archival restoration project for a cassette tape genealogical recording, the portable tape recorder (from the early 1970s) had a steady self-noise at 2.1 kHz. I grabbed a couple of the gates around that frequency and pulled them all the way up, ensuring reduction in that specific frequency band all the way through the track.

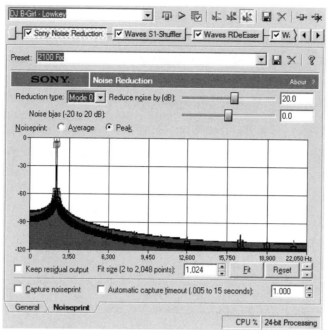

Noise Reduction as Notch Filter

Add a Dimension: The Waves S1 Stereo Imager

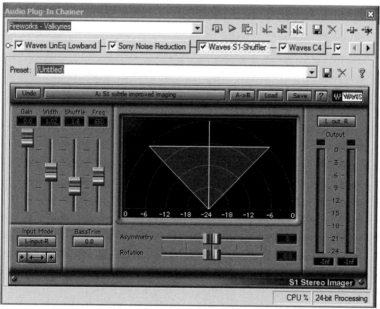

The Waves S1 Stereo Imager

The Waves S1 Stereo Imager provides a subtle broadening of the sound field in preparation for the enhancements coming up from the next processors. This part of the chain is also something that has to process the file "while it's young" and be applied before you take gain. This is a calm and subtle stage. However, after it goes through the Ultramaximizer, the subtle change becomes "more." The key to every stage prior to using the

Ultramaximizer is to neutralize the file as much as possible. You make it so that nothing is "sticking out": sibilance, boominess—these all need to be contained and calmed. Then when the file goes through the Ultramaximizer in a neutral state, everything becomes lush and large, without having something poke you in the eye.

Becoming Centered

Sometimes a track contains a vocal or lead instrument that belongs in the middle of the soundstage, but it is a bit heavy one way or the other; however, the right and left channels' stereo images are fine the way they are. The S1 provides a solution for this. It is also useful for tracks that are unbalanced in the stereo field, when one meter or the other has consistently higher levels. These solutions are implemented with the Asymmetry and Rotation controls.

The Rotation control lets you move the center of the sound left or right, and the Asymmetry control allows the left and right channels to be returned to their correct placement, while leaving the center tilted one way or the other. This is a great tool to use when the file is unbalanced in the stereo field. Using the Rotation control, move the triangle to the right or the left (to plus [right] or minus [left] 45 degrees), which results in an unbalanced triangle with a slanting top. Then, move the Asymmetry control to bring the top of the triangle back into a horizontal orientation, which returns the right and left channels to a proper balance and keeps the center material aimed where the center pointer is aimed in the stereo field—a very nifty trick!

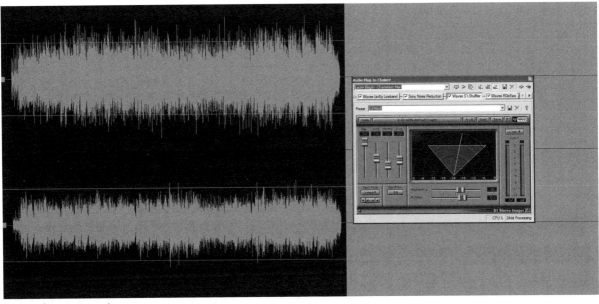

S1 Soundstage Correction

Mid-side Processing

Another function that the S1 provides is mid-side (M-S) processing. In mid-side, the left channel contains all the mono information (mid) and the right channel contains all the stereo information (side). Clicking on the Input Mode button toggles between L/R and M-S mode.

I recorded a jug band in my studio using a ribbon mic in figure-8 mode at some distance from the band, and a large-diaphragm condenser mic up close—just those two channels. It was remarkable that a happy accident occurred and I assigned these mono tracks into left and right stereo, with the condenser on the left and the figure-8 on the right. Engaging M-S on the track gave a solid center image and a wonderful stereo field; it was a fabulous solution, combining mixing and mastering in one step.

The S1 has another useful tool in its arsenal: the output meter can either show left/right signals (the default and usual use of the meter) or it can display mid-side information. By pressing the Out button above the meters, you can toggle between the standard stereo and mid-side monitoring. When M-S metering is in place, the meters display the *mid* (or mono component) level on the left, and the *side* (or stereo only) components on the right. This presents a great diagnostic tool to ensure that the file is properly phased—or to even detect a mono file.

With a mono file, just the left side of the M-S meter indicates level. A normal stereo file will have quite a bit of left (mono) side meter movement, and the right side will be softer and vary quite a bit with the stereo information. If the file is out of phase, the right side (stereo) will be very strong, and the left side (mono) will be variable. This metering is an alternative method of observing the signal only, and does not affect it in any way.

Solving Stereo Phase Issues

Another critical usage of the S1 is to easily detect and solve phase problems. Phase reversal is a relatively common and an often severe error. If one channel (or a significant part of a channel) is the opposite polarity to the other and the file is played in mono, the out-of-phase material will collapse in destructive interference and disappear from the audio. Audibly, out-of-phase material sounds hollow. If you shut one ear and put the open one in the center of your speaker system's sweet spot, you'll hear the bass disappear as each channel destructively interferes with the other.

If the file is out of phase, clicking one of the plus signs in the Input Mode section reverses the phase of one of the channels, returning the proper phase relationship to the file (don't select both, or you'll still have the same problem, but inverted.). The Input Mode section also solves the occasional swapped-channels problem: if left and right are obviously incorrect, clicking the double-headed arrow swaps the channels back.

Shuffling

The shuffling aspect of this plug-in widens the bass of the track and has no effect on the stereo imaging of mono or central components of the file. It enhances the existing stereo material without detrimental effect on overall mono compatibility. The way it works is to manipulate the levels and EQ of the mid and side signals. Increasing the side increases stereo width; applying complementary EQ shifts between the mid and the side generates the shuffling aspects of the processor. The QR code to the right leads to an article by the designer of the Shuffler, Michael Gerzon.

Michael Gerzon Stereo Shuffling Article

Leveraging the Chain

It is important to understand the leveraging effect that processors early in the plug-in chain have on later stages. Previously, we discovered that the Waves L3 Ultramaximizer made everything MORE when a file is processed with it: sibilance is more sibilant, boominess is boomier—very unsubtle. The key to tuning the Ultramaximizer with the plug-ins leading up to it is to use them to neutralize the file as much as possible, and then enhance the file while in its neutral state with the Ultramaximizer resulting in an appropriate and excellently mastered file.

Just like the butterfly effect in chaos theory, very small changes in initial conditions result in large changes down the road. In the same manner, very small changes in this and the following plug-ins have the most significant effect on the finished result. Because small changes make such big effects later, we are typically dealing in changes at these stages that are tenths of decibels. The S1 Stereo Imager is a good example of this. I've begun with the Subtle Improved Imaging preset, and (generally) only vary the Width control between 1.00 and 1.04 at most. That's it.

Get a Room: Reverb

We can add reverb to audio to create virtual room spaces, and very occasionally, that extra room is needed (but very subtly). The figure below shows a "roomy" room, but please note the Wet/Dry control: it is set to 2 percent wet. This is one of the rarest exceptions I make to the chain—there is usually a problem with too much reverb in a track. The C4 processor coming up next in the chain is all about expanding the sound and making little things in the background appear to be interesting features and "headphone dust" in the final track. Too much reverb on the premaster can totally wash out these subtleties, so beware. As a rather famous producer and mixer often says, "Fear Reverb."

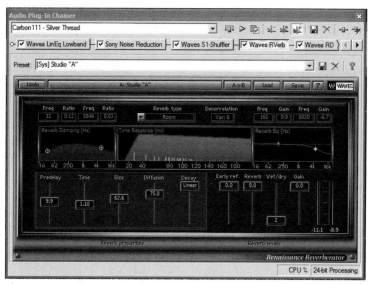

The Waves Renaissance Reverberator

Stop the Sibilance: The Waves Renaissance DeEsser

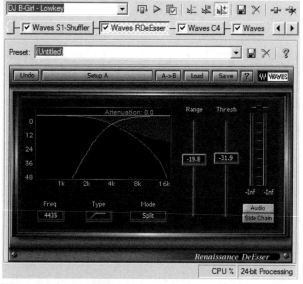

Waves Renaissance DeEsser

The Waves Renaissance DeEsser at this stage can be optional in the chain, depending on program material. It is placed just prior to the Waves C4 (which is the central control system of the mastering chain) and conditions the mid-high and high-frequency levels for presentation to the most critical mid-high band of the C4.

The DeEsser includes a crossover, which in my standard use splits the frequency range in two—high and low bands. The Freq (frequency) control sets the crossover point, allowing the low frequencies to pass and presents the high frequencies to a *sidechain*, which measures and compares the level of the high frequencies to the Threshold control, and if they are louder, attenuates (reduce) the high-frequency levels based on the Range setting.

This was a rare item in the chain until a couple of years ago, but now I am relying on it regularly. It fills a complementary function of the LinEQ Lowband at the beginning of the chain: where the LinEQ Lowband controls the low end, the DeEsser helps control the high end. I used to use it as a spot-sibilance solution—finding the precise frequency of the sibilance, setting the frequency here and using the notch filter "Type" of DeEsser. However, there were more examples of sibilance on the sonogram with no specific limited bandwidth frequency; oftentimes, the sibilant frequency would start at a typical 4 or 5 kHz range and go all the way up to 20 kHz, as in the following figure. These are the types of problems the Notch Filter mode doesn't handle very well. In the earlier days of using a multiband dynamics plug-in rather than the C4, I'd set the compression bandwidth to a wide setting, but that ended up being more noticeable. I finally figured out that when there is a significant short-term high-frequency burst (often sibilance), that clamping of the entire top end of the spectrum is acceptable, especially considering the function of the next plug-in in line—the Waves C4 Multiband Parametric Processor.

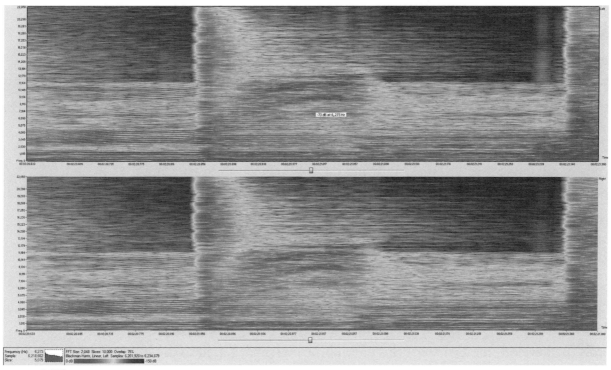

Tower of Sibilance

Always remember that in the mastering bundle of functionality, every component is strongly affected by the prior components in the chain. Each component sets the stage for the next. The de-esser, in this position, is conditioning and priming the upper midrange and high end of the C4, allowing the threshold and level settings in the C4 to be very subtle— tenths of decibels can and do make a significant difference in those critical articulation stages. Without the de-esser, those changes have to control a cruder, less homogenized signal.

How to Find Sibilant Frequencies

In the Waveform view of your workstation, zoom in on a sibilant section. This will appear as a very short, dense portion of the waveform like the one shown in the middle of the first figure below. Select this section and run an FFT/Sonogram on it. The sonogram of a selection that is this short looks like a series of horizontal lines across the screen—one of which is brighter than the rest, as shown in the second figure below. This bright line is likely to be your sibilant frequency (in this example, it is around 6.8 kHz). Use this frequency to set your de-esser notch filter, or, as is often the case, if there is a "tower" of sibilance showing in the sonogram as in the following figure, use the highpass sidechain type.

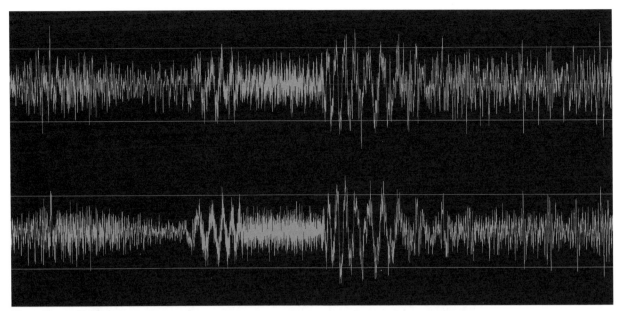

Short, Dense Sibilance

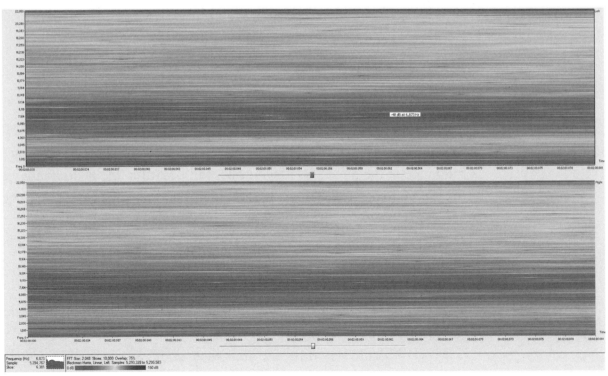

Sonogram of Sibilant Section

Balance and Strengthen: The Waves C4 Multiband Parametric Processor

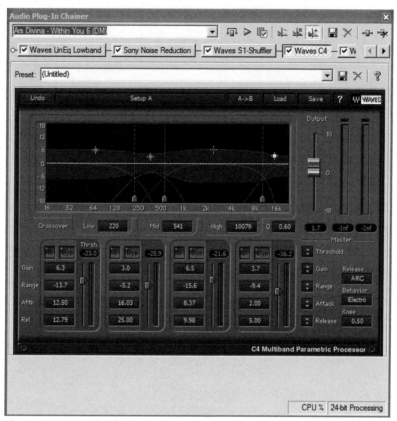

The Waves C4 Multiband Parametric Processor

Next in the chain is the Waves C4 Multiband Parametric Processor—my "secret weapon." This is where you take whatever gain is necessary to get full range of the meters for the output, and fine-tune the neutralizing of the file in preparation for the Ultramaximizer. The key to the C4 is the bouncing yellow line that displays the instantaneous EQ (Waves calls it DynamicLine), whose motion is based on the Threshold, Gain, and Range control settings.

With the C4 you are primarily calibrating the ballistics, vectors, and dynamics of each frequency band. Again, at this stage of the chain, little changes make big changes downstream.

My settings are very different from what comes as a mastering default in the plug-in. The biggest difference is the attack and release (in the bass section): I have them set very fast. The secret to setting the C4 (and consequently the entire mastering chain) lies in ballistics and dynamics—that is, how fast and how far each component frequency is allowed (or encouraged) to move. The following figure shows a system default "mastering" setting.

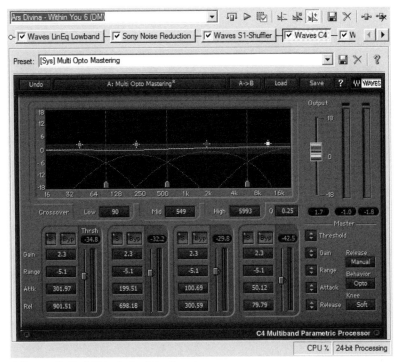

A System Default "Mastering" C4 Preset

The C4 Frequency Ranges

There are four frequency ranges that the C4 processes in the desktop mastering chain: bass, low mids, upper mids, and the top octave. The C4 begins its processing as a three-way crossover, a function that separates and routes each frequency range to a separate set of controls. This is very educational as there is a Solo (S) button in each band. You can learn a lot by listening carefully to each band soloed.

At the end of its processing, the C4 delivers a recombined full-range signal to the next plug-in in the chain. Each separated section behaves as a compressor (or expander) for its respective frequencies, with the common settings of Threshold, Attack, and Release for each band.

The Bass Section

In the bass section, one distinct change in my standard setting from the system default settings (300 to 500 ms) for the C4 is the release times (*especially* in the bass section), which I have set very fast (12 ms); this results in punchy and defined bass with a lot of movement in it. This section covers the low-end range of 20 Hz to 220 Hz, is set to Compand (compress and/or expand, depending on the threshold setting), and is set for a wide range of motion.

The Lower Midrange

The lower midrange covers the frequency range of 220 Hz to 550 Hz—what I used to call the "TV speaker sound," based on the early days of television when there was just a small tinny speaker in television sets. Now, with full-range surround-sound hi-fi systems, that is no longer an apt description. These days, we'd call it "laptop sound." Eventually, I'm sure, fine audio will be reproduced everywhere, so we can call this range the "muffled" sound range. The appropriate setting for this range is clamped and controlled—pinched. One of the only situations in which I let this range expand quite a bit is when I need to hear a more "throaty" sound from vocals. Again, audition this range with the solo button to get a good sense of what is happening here.

The Upper Midrange

The upper midrange of the C4 is the most critical band in the entire desktop mastering chain. This section is where the articulation and intelligibility of a file resides. Ultimately, it is where the majority of your polishing work is done (with granularity of tenths of decibels), and it contains the most important set of controls in the entire plug-in chain. This section covers the 550 Hz to 10 kHz frequency range and, like the low end, is set to Compand—however, during the majority of the time this section is acting as an Expander.

The Top Octave

The top octave covers the range of 10 kHz to 20 kHz, in which only the highest tinny sounds exist. These frequencies are the sprinkles on the cake, and like the low mid, this range is clamped and controlled.

Calibrating Ballistics, Vectors, and Dynamics

Besides attack and release, which I rarely change, there are three ways to control each band. The Gain control moves the upper range of the purple area up or down in decibels, which controls the expansion amount of low-level (under the threshold) signals. During the softest sections, the instantaneous EQ shown by the yellow DynamicLine rides the upper curve set by the Gain control, as shown below.

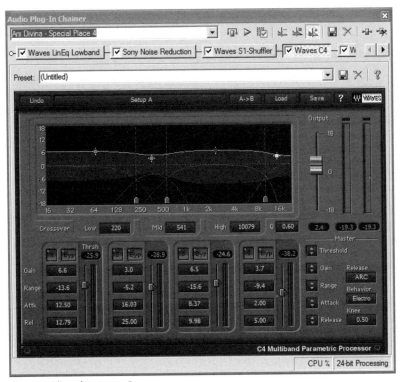

The C4 Riding the Upper Curve

The Threshold control modifies the ballistics (whether the yellow line "favors" the top or bottom end of the range).

The Range control sets the bottom extremes of the purple area. This curve defines compression limits during the loudest sections of the file (even though, unlike the Gain setting, the signal rarely hits the absolute bottom of the Range limit; see the C4 image in figure below, showing a time-lapse image across a whole file, exhibiting that the majority of processing is expansion and the DynamicLine generally stays above the 0 dB line). In the upper midrange section, this works as a true de-esser, allowing the yellow line to sink farther on loud transients. This lower curve of the purple area being set by the Range control is really where de-essing is controlled; lowering this Range value increases the depth of the purple area and makes the DynamicLine bounce farther into compression. This is the heart of where ballistics (how fast and how deep the line moves) are set.

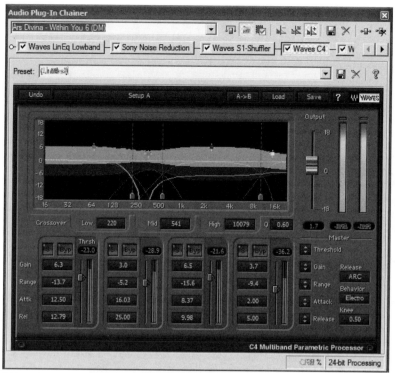

A Time-Lapse Demonstration of the Preponderance of Expansion in the C4

The vertically symmetric "fish" shape of the C4 settings is critical to the success of the desktop mastering plug-in chain design, and is the core feature of my "sound."

When there is audio running through the plug-in, the representative level of each band shows up in the respective sets of meters. When the metered audio reaches the Threshold control indicator, the yellow line "instantaneous EQ" is halfway between the higher Gain setting and the lower Range setting. Since the Gain and Range settings shown here are vertically mirror-imaged around the zero point, the output for the section is at unity gain when the audio levels are at the Threshold indicator—in other words, the same level is output from the band as came into it.

When the meter indicators rise above the Threshold setting, the yellow line pushes down (causing compression), and if the meter indicator is below, or softer than, the Threshold setting, the yellow line rises (causing expansion). At silence (or close to it), the yellow line rests along the top of the purple area defined by the Gain setting. See the following figure.

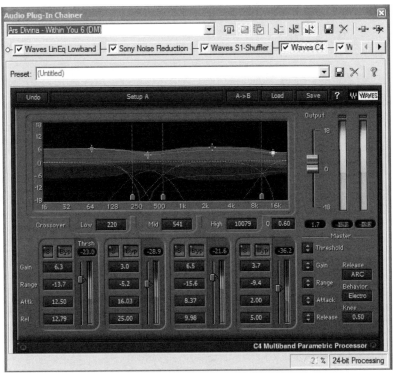

A Lighter Time-Lapse Showing Optimal C4 Threshold Settings

Thresholds can be thought of as a level control for each band, and should be set near the top of the average meter deflection in each band's Threshold section. This sets the average position of the DynamicLine at 0 dB (typically, unity gain). Then, while listening to the track, use the Threshold controls as subtle volume controls for each band.

It is interesting to watch the deflection and motion of the DynamicLine, especially in the upper mids. On screen if you just look at the purple range of the upper mids and the line usually following the midpoint, it can appear like lips and a mouth. I've noticed that when the controls are set properly, the animation of the line appears to "sing" at you. The louder sounds deflect the line lower in the range, and quietness closes up the "mouth."

If there is quite a bit of song-to-song level deviation in your project, you'll likely hear it in the threshold settings of the C4 first. If the current track being mastered is much softer than the last one (using the previous plug-in chain settings as a starting point for this track), you'll hear more high end. This is due to the C4 thresholds being set higher for the previous track, and delivering more expansion than compression. As a quick fix, you can bring all the Thresholds down at once (with the ganged

Threshold control) till the brightness evens out, and then continue fine-tuning each band for the current track.

Often there are more significant changes from song to song, such as vocal placement in the stereo field. When you make significant changes for a given track in the plug-in chain, save it as a new preset (this would be a "branch of the tree"). Then, return to the initially saved chain to begin the next track. If there aren't significant changes from track to track, using the previous track's presets as the starting point on the next track provides some continuity across the record. It is a good idea to master the tracks in their final CD order, if the order has been determined.

If the track is too bright, try bringing the DeEsser (just previous in the chain) Thresh control down a bit. This can help smooth out the high end overall. If quiet sections are not bright enough, raise the Gain setting in the upper-mid section of the C4. When you do raise the Gain settings in the C4, be sure to pull down the Range setting to keep the purple area generally centered around the 0 dB line.

When the balance is right, select the proper make-up gain level with the C4 Output control. Depending on the intensity of the track, this is where you'll take most of the gain—usually bringing the output meters all the way to the top, staging the gain in preparation for the L3 Ultramaximizer, coming up next.

Make Everything MORE: The Waves L3 Ultramaximizer

The Waves L3 Ultramaximizer is another "secret weapon" in my arsenal, and the tool that ultimately makes desktop mastering possible. The L3 provides look-ahead limiting (reading ahead in the file for clipping and lowering the level of the clipped waveforms down to the Out Ceiling level setting).

Compressors and limiters are fundamentally automatic volume controls. When a level gets too loud (defined by the Threshold control), a compressor will turn that volume down (usually defined by the

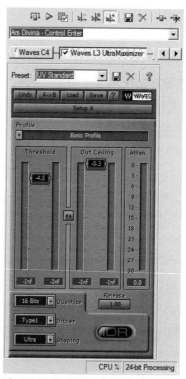

The Waves L3 Ultramaximizer

Ratio control, and sometimes preset into the plug-in). A Limiter, on the other hand, keeps turning the volume down at loud sounds so the output is a given level and no higher. These are typically followed by a make-up gain stage, which brings the overall level up. This is the purpose of the Output Gain stage in the C4, where we set the level to provide the L3 with the largest input we can before clipping. If we allow a soft level to go into the L3, we are not using all the resolution available to us.

The L3 Threshold at −4.5 and the Out Ceiling at −0.3 are pretty constant. On rare occasions, if the track needs to be quiet and noticeably uncompressed, the L3 Threshold can be raised to −2.5, and on rare occasions that you need a track to slam, the Threshold can drop as far as −4.9, but I wouldn't go much past that. The L3 is where you can lose your dynamic range by overdoing it—that is, when all the instruments appear to be the same level. We are really trying to tune for the standard setting of the L3 in the majority of projects.

The Ultramaximizer is what I was told "mastering is" when I looked for answers at the beginning of my mastering career. It can make everything MORE. If you have sibilance or boominess, the Ultramaximizer aggravates the condition, but if you have smoothed everything out, the Ultramaximizer truly makes the track shine.

Previously, at the de-esser stage, we were "preprocessing" the high end, taking a lot of the bulk out of the signal, in the same way that we did at the beginning with the LinEQ Lowband when we took a lot of bulk out of the low end. It is important that the de-esser comes after the noise reduction, so the high end is still sparkly, and after the stereo imaging, so the file is moving and enhanced. The chain up to the point of the C4 has now contained and tamed the file to provide a single set of controls: the upper midrange "articulation area" of the C4.

Quantization, Dither, and Noise Shaping

The L3 Ultramaximizer provides additional critical functionality besides look-ahead limiting. It is the last plug-in in the chain for a good reason: quantization, dither, and noise shaping make up the final process in the enhancement of the original premastered track.

Quantization

Quantization is the function of reducing the binary word length to a less resolved state: 24-bit to 16-bit, for example. In an analog-to-digital converter, the fully resolved analog signal is split up into *quanta*—discrete packets of information. These packets are each given values and stored.

These values are, by definition, less resolved than the original analog signal. In mastering, we take a given input, manipulate and process it, and generate a given output. Ideally our input is at a much higher resolution than our output, so we don't have to create information that does not exist. We are enhancing what is already there and delivering more highly refined content to a lower state, be that a 16-bit .wav file or a compressed MP3 file.

Using the Seattle to Austin metaphor, a quantizer takes the samples that are on the 6-inch marks (24 bits) and intelligently moves them to the 142-foot marks (16 bits). The intelligence that drives the decisions of which 142-foot mark to choose is called *dithering*.

Dither

Remember that the 142-foot marks in a 24-bit file live in the 9th bit. In a 24-bit file, you can think of three 8-bit sections. The section of 8 bits on the right is the least significant section—it can define only 256 different values. The 8-bit section in the middle provides numerical ranges from 256 to 65,536 values. And the most significant section, on the left, defines values from 65,536 to 16,777,216. When quantizing a 24-bit file to a 16-bit file, the 8 bits in the right section are all given the value of zero. The big part that dither plays is in deciding the value of that 9th bit. After the file is quantized and dithered, the least-significant 8 bits with the zero value can be thrown away, or "truncated," and you are left with the desired 16-bit file.

Without dither, the choice of which value (zero or one) to set the least significant bit to can result in a long series of zeros or ones, which may form something that looks like a periodic square wave. That, in turn, can result in an audible form of distortion called "quantization distortion."

To avoid quantization distortion, a dither rule is used to set a zero or one on a semirandom basis based on probability, which boils down to "if you've gone *this* direction too many times in a row, go *that* direction." This adds a bit of low-level noise that is visible in the workstation and audible, but not as disturbing as quantization distortion.

A Good Dither Explanation

Take a decaying acoustic-guitar note, for example: without dither, the long decay of the note into silence ends with a bit of a buzz (quantization distortion); but with dither on, the note fades off into the noise, and gives the appearance of resolving better than the resolution could support.

It is important to understand that this example is one in which you can actually hear the quantization and dither phenomenon, but the activity is going on in the selection of the least significant bit no matter what the overall level of the file is at any given time. It works on all least significant bits in loud as well as soft sections.

Noise Shaping

All of the DSP processes up to this point in the chain have generated unavoidable obligatory (by the physical rules of digital signal processing) broadband noise in the signal. These physical rules have a loophole, fortunately—you must have the noise generated by DSP in your audio, but you are allowed to shove it into the high-frequency closet.

What noise shaping does is to take that unavoidable broadband noise and stack it up at 19 kHz. This is such a high frequency that most people don't even hear it, so a bit of noise there is usually inaudible. This leaves the rest of the frequency range "cleaner than it can possibly be," according to the DSP rules. However, as soon as you do one more digital process to the signal, that broadband noise returns to the signal, with the addition of the lump of noise up at 19 kHz (which you can see as a "cloud" on a sonogram—that's how you can tell if something has been noise shaped).

The Very Best Reference Work for DSP

Watch What You're Doing: The Waves PAZ Analyzer

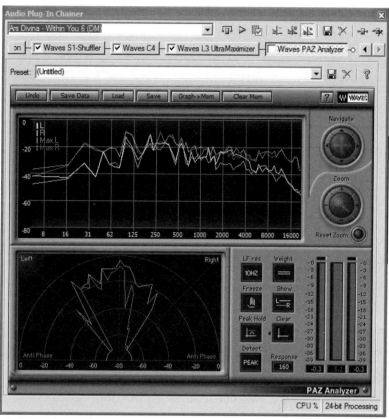

The Waves PAZ Analyzer

The last plug-in in my chain is the Waves PAZ Analyzer. This is another informative tool regarding frequency ranges and stereo phases. Notice that I have this plug-in bypassed: the PAZ Analyzer has no effect on the sound of the audio, so there is no reason to have it actively in the audio path. That is a general rule of thumb with any and all processing modules and settings—if you aren't using them, turn them off.

Postmastering Processes

Now that the mastering is complete and you are happy with the results, ask yourself these questions to make sure that the mastered track is right. Any of these issues are okay if you meant for them to be that way.

- Does the file use the full resolution (or appropriate amount) of the display? If not, perhaps it is not compressed enough. This is a highly variable criterion—you don't want soft acoustic guitar and vocals to be as loud and big as a heavy rock track.

- Does the intention of the track show through? Do you resonate with the music, so you really get what the artist is going for? Is it musical? A good test of this is if it is hard to stop the song while it is running. Usually it's very easy to stop an unmastered track. I've had to throw in my mastering chain just to begin to listen to some work.

- Does the mastered track generally match the rest of the songs in the project? This goes back to intention—you are the last person to ensure that the complete vision of the artist is realized. Have a good feeling about track-to-track level, while keeping in mind that the ballads should be quieter than the anthems.

- Is it too compressed, or loglike? This can easily sneak up on you and happen, and may masquerade as being too much if it is a very long song that is zoomed way out. Make sure that you zoom in on different places in the track and verify that the soft parts are still soft during the loud sections. That is the core of the concept of dynamic range.

- Is there a channel imbalance? This can sneak up on you as well. Sometimes the mastering exacerbates a problem that wasn't so evident in the premaster.

If the track passes all the items on this list, you are probably ready to go on to the next stage, tops and tails.

Cleanup: Tops and Tails

Once you are sure the track is ready, the following steps are very important to do in order.

The file that results from running the plug-in chain (if it was a 24-bit file to begin with) will still be a 24-bit file, but with the 8 least-significant-bits set to zero. This makes for a very interesting file, and one that caused me a lot of confusion when I first ran across it. The figure below shows the fully zoomed in, (very) low-level sample view. What is interesting about this is the sample values are multiples of 256: 256, 512, 768! When I first saw this, I thought something was wrong. We had run a 16-bit file into an Alesis Masterdisc set at 24-bit, and I was sure there was a mistake. But it became very clear—the 16-bit source file was just padded out with zeros, and that is what we have here.

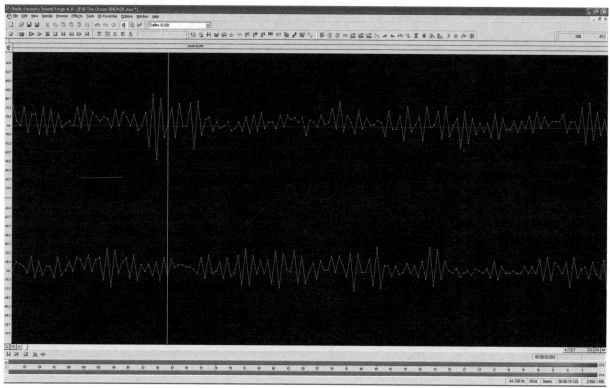

A 16-bit Quantized 24-bit File

Next, use your software to truncate the file to 16-bit. This collapses all the 256 multiples into standard linear numbering, as in the following image. Now it is truly a 16-bit file in every way. There is a potential error that lies in wait for you if you add fades—tops and tails—to the file before truncation. Since the file is still 24-bit, the 16-bit quantization collapses into linear sample values in the fade sections. Truncating after this process loses the intelligent quantization provided by the dither and noise shaping.

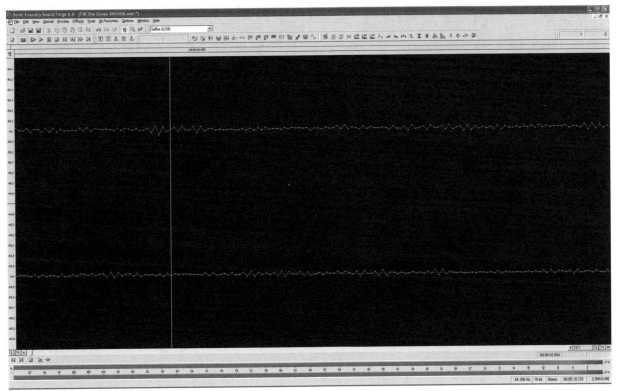

A Truncated 16-bit File

Now that you are in the proper file format, you are ready for the next stage of cleanup, which is deleting the two-second start noise at the beginning of the track you added to ensure that the thresholds were all crossed. I found it valuable to create a macro that would delete these first two seconds.

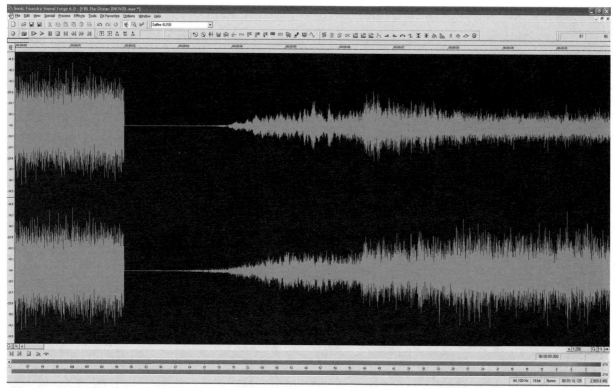

Tops Start with Noise

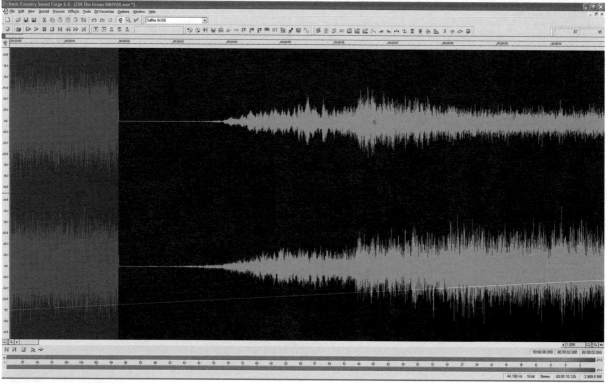

Tops Start with Noise Selected

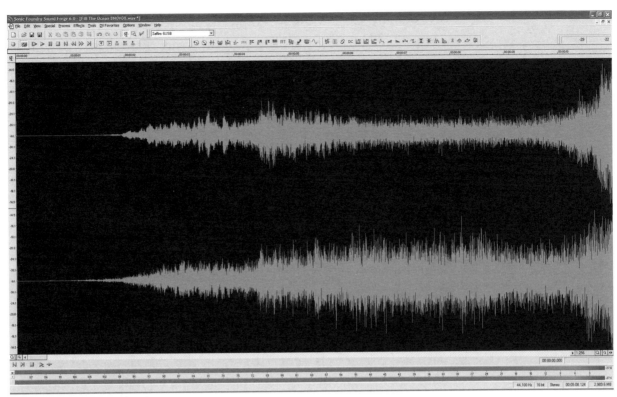

Tops Start with Noise Deleted

In Sony Creative Software's Sound Forge, these are the keystrokes:

Press Ctrl + G (for Go To), press Shift + ; and then press 2 (this goes to two seconds), press Enter (this actually takes you there), press Ctrl + Shift + Home (this selects from your current location to the start of the file), and press Delete (which deletes the selection).

Make sure that your units (seconds, samples, frames) are the same as when you recorded your macro. It can be unexpected to delete just the first two samples of the file.

Tops

After the start noise has been deleted, select the appropriate amount of time for the *lead-in* (the top). This is something that you get better at with experience. The more you listen to music, the better you'll get at these tasks, and the right values will sound "right."

To set the fade-in, zoom the resolution to the first notes of the file horizontally, and zoom in full vertically. This is a great place to see if you remembered to switch the file from 24- to 16-bit—the vertical zoom makes it obvious by the spiky nature of the samples (see the previous image of a 16-bit quantized 24-bit file). Often, linear fades are acceptable for the tops, but sometimes you'll want a graphic fade to mask some unpleasantness in the beginning.

Occasionally songs will have count-ins or clicks to start the track, and the artist should be clear with you about whether these should stay in the final mastered track. Generally, I discourage the idea because it can sound unprofessional. Consider all the listens of all the people there will be to this track; do you want them to wait through a count-in each time they listen to the song? Again, if the opinion to keep the clicks or the count is a considered one, then more power to you—but beware of "demo-itis," where the artist has listened to a piece in a certain way so often that they fall in love with an early version. It happens to me all the time.

The next step in processing tops is to choose the part of the file that is typically just before the beginning attack, and then delete to the start. Now, hit Play (usually with the Spacebar), and see how the start feels. Often it can be too abrupt, and you'll need to undo the deletion and select a little earlier in the file for the beginning. Start times for tracks vary depending on the music or content type. Test different timings until the start of the song feels right. "Right," in this case, is how it feels when the song should come in after you hit Play on a CD player. This sets the top duration.

When you make your selection of the beginning of the song, include a few cycles of the first *transient*, the first bit of the meat of the song, as shown below. While fading in, the inclusion of the first bit of the beginning of the track blends the fade, like blending paints in a painting.

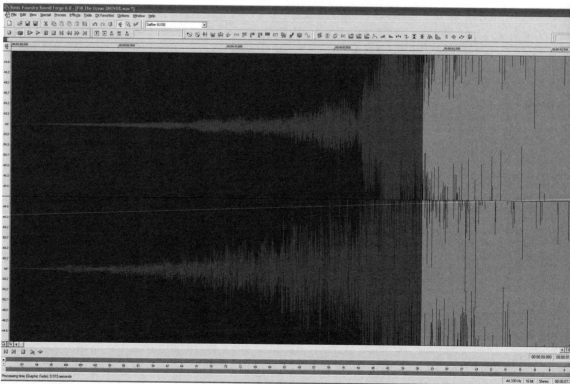

Tops Selection

The start interval is dependent on the starting envelope of the program material. A long attack calls for a nonabrupt beginning, a quick start calls for a shorter beginning. Beware the CD unmuting time; if your beginning is too short, it is possible to have the first part of the sound cut off, depending on the CD player used for playback.

Next, choose a graphic fade to bring the file from absolute silence. It is critical that tracks (or loops) start and end with "the speaker at rest." Otherwise, snaps and clicks may ensue.

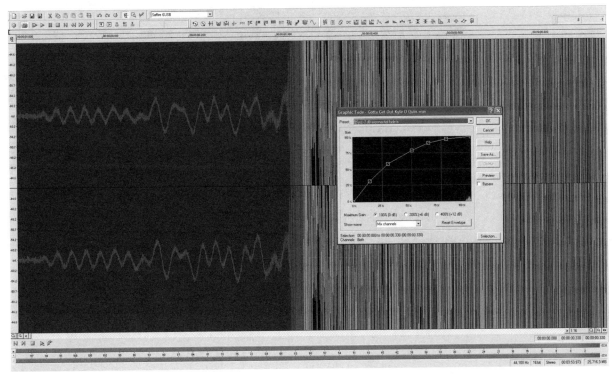

A 3 dB Graphic Fade-In

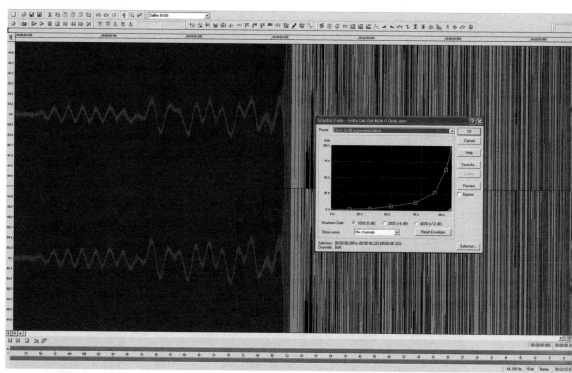

A 20 dB Graphic Fade-In

Shorter attacks, like snare drumbeats or big beginning chords need a more shaped graphic fade. When you apply a fade, listen to it several times for naturalness. If the beginning of the song has a long fade-in, you may want to select from the start of the file to halfway up the length of the attack and apply a linear fade.

When the top is taken care of, go to the end of the file and repeat a similar process to set the tail.

Tails

Fade-outs, or tails, have a couple of purposes: first, to ensure that the end of the song is fully silent—the loudspeaker at rest, and second, to mask potential low-level issues, like unintended tape punch-out clicks, chair squeaks, and other noises. It also masks other issues potentially generated by the mastering chain, such as low-level robotic or mechanical noise-reduction artifacts and other muting factors that muddy the low-level sound.

The more naturally that the end time of the track is set, the easier sequencing becomes, since the tracks will be appropriately timed to begin with. Don't cut the tails off too early—you'll notice the low-level noise that the noise shaping leaves at the end of the file, and you'll want that to smoothly blend to zero.

Sometimes you need to cover blemishes with tops and tails: for instance, if the noise reduction leaves too much residue at the fade-out, you can cover it up with a tasteful graphic fade. There are several graphic fade types. The 6 dB (top left below) and 3 dB fades (top right below) are common, a fast fade is handy (bottom left below), and I've been using an in-between 6 and 3 dB curve (bottom right below) with good results. Tops and tails need to be set with a nice even slope, with no sharp discontinuities. These are some of the artistic aspects of being a mastering engineer.

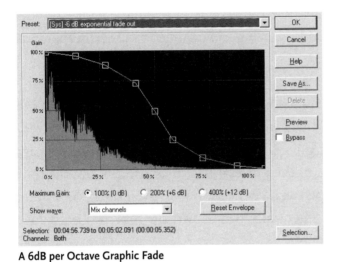

A 6dB per Octave Graphic Fade

A 3dB per Octave Graphic Fade

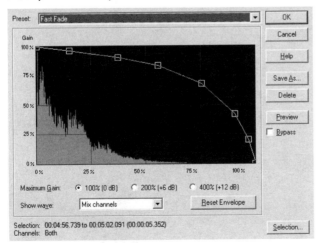

A Fast Fade

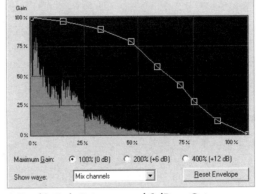

A Graphic Fade Between 3 and 6 dB per Octave

Fading Out Repeating Sections

You'll often be asked to add a fade-out to repeating choruses at the end of a track, and sometimes you'll be given tracks with many repeats at the end and will have to determine the appropriate length of the finished track. Obviously, you wouldn't want a song to end in the middle of a line or a hook, so there is a process to identify the musically correct number of repeats that a given outro should have.

The figure below shows the end of a track with many repeats, with the last three chosen as the fade. To select an appropriate fade, find the key that inserts markers in your software and play the song. As each repeating outro chorus begins, hit the key and place the marker. Now you'll see the structure of the end of the song, and be able to make the choice of how long or short to make the fade, starting and ending on musically appropriate sections.

In rock and pop music, letting something repeat four times is generally appropriate. Remember, your job as mastering engineer is to determine what the rest of the world will hear every time that the song is played. Make sure they love it. I regularly get songs to master that I may not care for at first, but by the end of the process, after mastering, I love them. If you don't or can't find a personal connection to a given track, be willing to talk to the artist and potentially turn down the job. You must love your work.

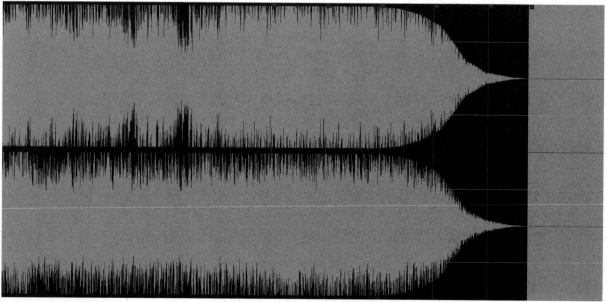

Looping Outro Markers

The Human Lens

Another quality-control practice for finished tracks is what I call the *human lens*, the idea that when you play your work for other people, the feedback you are looking to receive isn't based on how they are responding or reacting to your work—rather, it's based on how you feel about them listening to the project. You are, in essence, listening through their ears. This can be a good personal indicator of how happy you are with a given piece.

Mastered File Management and Delivery

Now that the track is fully complete, it's time to save it into the Complete subdirectory of the artist-name directory. I prefer to use the following file-naming standard format: Artist_Name-Song_Name_Mastered_DDMMYY.wav. The underscores instead of spaces allow the file to travel into all the potential backwood areas of the Internet that might have issues with spaces (spaces show up as "%20" in html addresses, and are unsightly). The figure below shows the Save As dialog box with a couple of files already completed. A nice time-saver is to copy the current song name into the clipboard, select one of the existing track's file names in the dialog box to capture the full structure of the file name with the artist and date already set up, then paste the current song_name from the clipboard at the appropriate place in the file name.

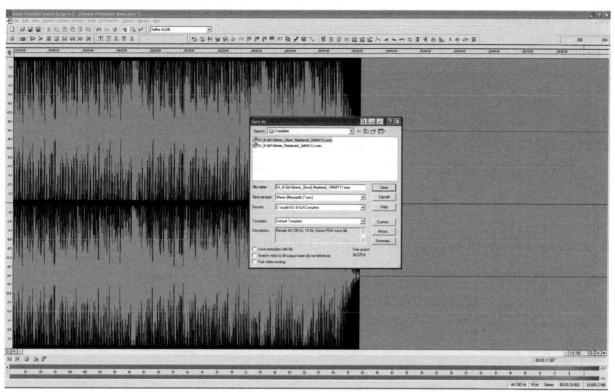

Save As Dialog Box

When all the files for the day and for the artist are mastered and saved, open the Complete directory and generate MP3s from the mastered .wav files. I use a program called dBpoweramp Music Converter from Illustrate. It is a Windows program that integrates into the Windows shell, allowing right-click access to convert practically any format of audio file into practically any other format of audio file. I use the LAME 192 Constant Bit Rate conversion, and this software lets me select a whole directory full of files for processing at one time.

dBpoweramp Music Converter from Illustrate

Now that you have your .wav and MP3 files, the next step is to send them back to the client. I use YouSendIt Express for this: a program that runs locally to interface with the yousendit.com file-transfer website. It also integrates into the Windows shell, so I just have to select all the files I want to send, right-click and choose "Send by YouSendIt," and a dialog box pops up asking for the recipient's e-mail address with a subject and message field.

If this is a standalone project (not aimed for creating a Production Master CD [PMCD]), then on receipt of the files my clients send me $50 per track via PayPal. This turns into a nice way to spend your days! Otherwise, we carry on to the sequencing stage to create the PMCD and Listening Copy CD.

7

Sequencing and Production Master CDs

When you sequence an album, you take all the songs and line them up one after another (using Sony CD Architect, in my setup). Sequencing is one of the most creative steps of the mastering process. It is your time to assemble all the parts (tracks) into the "big song" that is the album that fans will grow to love (hopefully!). This can be done alone or with the producer or group, depending on the circumstances of the job.

Sequencing

Usually a band or a project has a desired track running order for its CD. Sometimes, a more enjoyable and rewarding method of setting a song order is to let a given song "ask" for the next song. By listening to the end of a given track, and the beginnings of the songs that are up for sequencing, you can hear which ones fit together well.

Track Spacing and the Snap Game

There are generally three ways of spacing and setting the time between songs in a musical way: by beat, by breath, or as a palette cleanser. Typically, the songs will tell you when you have it right, and things will sound noticeably wrong if not.

■ Spacing *by beat* is just that—counting along with the beats at the end of the track and coming in on the 1, or a related musically pleasing timing, in order to connect the two songs.

- Spacing *by breath* is when a noticeable tempo, tone, or tuning change happens between the two songs and the last song needs to resonate in the mind of the listener. It is accomplished literally by taking a deep breath at the end of one song and releasing it, and then starting the next song.

- Spacing *as a palette cleanser* is used between "sides" of an album or as a buffer for an even more jagged change between two tracks. With this change mode, it is a "wait until it feels right" action.

This brings us to the "snap game." This is a method that can be used during sequencing when the artist(s) and/or producers are attending the sequencing session. The trick is to have everyone listen to the end of the song (while not watching the screen) and snap their fingers (or clap if their snap is weak) when they feel the next song should start. This is usually great fun, and revealing of the physiology of rhythm in artists and creative types.

Sequencing is also the time when you can try out crossfades and transitions that can potentially look and sound *really* wrong but can often be quite interesting. And for that reason, they regularly end up on the finished disc.

One challenge with deep crossfades is that the start and end times of the track, when ripped as a single song, will cut off abruptly. This won't be a problem with individual-track digital distribution, but if the CD is played on shuffle it can be disconcerting.

This act of sequencing is the laying out of the uber-meta-song and is one of the biggest joys in mastering; it is one of the overlooked joys of the full music-creation process. This is the stage at which you make the music that people fall in love with and to. It creates the overarching song of the full album, and is ideally timed in such a way that you not only don't want to turn the music off, but you have the desire to repeat the experience over and over.

One of the sad requests I (rarely) get is to use the stock two-second interval spacing, which is usually insisted upon because it's "supposed to be that way." Using this type of spacing often prevents an opportunity for an additional stage of beauty for the listener, by losing the crossfades and musical timing available to guide the listener from song to song, enhancing the act of listening to the record.

There are exceptions to this desired artistic assembly of the CD, such as on instructional discs, with licensed music, and with CDs for radio single airplay exclusively. But one of the true joys of listening to albums is the flow and cross-flow of the songs.

Sequencing is also when the artist and song meta-data for the album is set, any CD-TEXT is burned onto the disc in subcodes, and ISRC codes are assigned to each song.

ISRC Codes

ISRC (International Standard Recording Code) codes are globally unique identifiers for each track, similar to UPC codes that are used for the full physical CD. These codes are built from four subcodes:

ISRC Info

1. Country Code
2. Registrant (Agent) Code
3. Year of Reference Code
4. Designation Code

The only globally unique portion of these codes is the *agent code*: for instance, my UltraViolet Studios code is GTJ. So for the 200th song that I master in 2012, the ISRC will read US-GTJ-12-00200. Since each agent code is unique, the system ensures that there are no duplications of numbers.

The agent code is requested from and delivered by the RIAA. It is a good idea to keep track of the ISRC codes that you have assigned in a spreadsheet, as shown in the in the ISRC Spreadsheet Example following.

ISRC Spreadsheet Example

A CD Architect 5.0 Cautionary Tale

Moving from CD Architect 4.5 (a plug-in type of program that worked inside Sony Sound Forge 4) to CD Architect 5.0, Sonic Foundry's (at that time, later Sony) first attempt at a standalone CD-mastering application came with some undesired changes. One of the new features was the ability for the end user to pull any types of digital files together and burn them to a CD. In order to "protect" these novice users, the decision was made to provide a dither algorithm in a plug-in chain by default on opening new files. In addition to that decision, the company decided to conceal the feature, docking it in a place that was hidden—also by default. This dither, coming after the final mastered, noise-shaped files, had a significantly detrimental effect on the quality of the playback.

This caused quite a bit of trouble until I figured it out with a tech-support call, in which I asked why the same track that was played in CD Architect sounded much worse than in Sound Forge directly. So, know be sure to know which "defaults" your software has engaged to protect novices.

Sequencing Workflow

To begin a new session in CD Architect, delete the default master plug-in chain (one solution to this is to save a cleared version as a template to start new sessions with). Then, save the file as your project file name; it is good practice to name the file with the artist name, album name, and date.

Use the Explorer to select the files for the CD. If you can, get a full list of the song titles in a spreadsheet format from the artist. You can select the file order from the list, and when the time comes to fill out the song titles for the CD-TEXT, you can copy and paste whole columns at once.

Once you have all the songs selected and the artist name and song titles entered into the metadata fields of your software, you can copy the "Artist" and "Song Title" columns to your ISRC spreadsheet. Auto-fill the ISRC numbers and copy them back to the ISRC column in the CD Architect application.

One useful benefit of CD Architect is that you can Save As a CD Architect .wav file and render the entire CD as a single .wav file. The advantage of this is that if you open a CD Architect .wav file in CD Architect, all program markers and attributes of the session come along. This makes it great to share and check projects, and the software is very inexpensive considering its utility.

8

Real World Mastering Applications

In this chapter I'd like to share with you the variety of projects that I've had the good fortune to work on in my career to date. I'll also recommend several starting points you can use for your own career.

The universe makes the setlist, so being open to the variety of options and opportunities that come in provides for endless entertainment. I have a steady stream of work that is generated via word of mouth from clients, but a good measure comes in from appropriate visibility and "performances" on social networks (I'll get into more depth about that in chapter 9, "Mastering as a Business").

As a teenager, I was criticized for buying too many records, often to the end of not having enough money for food (my best friend's mother would say "Eat your records!" when I'd ask for a snack). I was also told that I was buying records just to impress my friends. These were challenges to my most inner self, and a realization presented itself: music and records would be my lifelong career, and my obsession with music and devouring records were worthy investments into that career. I am happy to announce that that reading turned out to be correct, and can say that following your passion can be a rewarding endeavor.

Options and Opportunities

The first step for the aspiring mastering engineer is to have an enjoyable practice and learn the craft. There are many ways to do this independently. You don't need clients to begin with—you can be your own client!

There are three reasons to take a job: for the money, for the connections, or for the fun of it. In the early days of your career, this will probably play out in reverse order. Start by having fun, next make as many connections as you can, and then you can begin making money. Here are some ideas, from the most independent to the most unlikely.

Capture and Master Your Favorite Records and Tapes

I recommend capturing and mastering your favorite records; this is something you don't have to wait for. Hopefully you have access to a record player or tape player and a music digitizing system (sound card). It's okay if the music you capture doesn't sound too good right off the bat; that is what your mastering practice is for. As you develop your process, you can offer to capture and master favorite LPs and cassettes for other people.

Select tracks from various sources—records, CDs, cassettes—anything you can find (and personally love). Take these tracks and work on making them as consistent with each other as possible, as if they were from the same release. Then, make a compilation CD.

Not every record has been released as a CD or into the digital marketplace yet—this can be a good example of listening for work. Talk to older people that were music lovers in the vinyl era and offer to capture their favorite albums.

I've become Facebook friends with many of my musical heroes, and have been so bold as to share my personally mastered restored versions of their work. Sometimes they've been excited enough to hire me. This is a good thing, but sometimes I'm sure it was unwelcome. Develop a keen sense of when you are about to go too far in self-promotion, and respect that sense.

Music Programs in High Schools and Colleges

Local music programs in high schools and colleges often need support from the community, and that's you. The great thing about interacting with students is that many can become friends and clients, potentially for life. Another subset will succeed in attaining their dreams and will be grateful to those that helped them with that success—that can also be you.

As your career progresses, you'll be able to share your knowledge with others. Offer to be a guest speaker about mastering (or whatever your specialization is). Forging productive relationships with music teachers and administrators provides resounding value for all concerned.

I had the opportunity to teach audio recording at Shoreline Community College in Seattle (2001 through 2002), where they had a student group called the Sonic Arts Club. A few years later they wanted to make and sell a CD of their work as a fund-raiser. Keeping in touch with the students brought my services to their mind first, and I came to one of their meetings and described appropriate mixing for mastering. Then, they came to my studio in small groups and we mastered each of their tracks. Finally, we sequenced and released the CD.

This didn't generate a lot of income at the time, but it helped a couple of dozen aspiring engineers to see their work in the context of the bigger recording picture, and many of those students did return to me for future work. Additionally, I regularly get calls from out of the blue to master albums, and when I ask who referred them to me, it often turns out to be a former student.

Teen Center Studios

There are a couple of teen centers around Seattle that have recording studios in them, and in the early days of my practice, I dropped off stacks of business cards at each one, offering my work. The counselors and administrators passed these cards to the bands, and there was more work. These, of course, were low-paying projects, but I was fulfilling my heart's desire!

Professional Compilation Albums

Mastering and sequencing compilation albums is one of the best ways to broaden your market. Follow your desires and focus on the type of music you most enjoy. Seek out and befriend (via social media or otherwise) others who share your love for your favorite type of music. Fan clubs and festivals are worthy contact and networking points. Find the person responsible for getting things done, and offer to help them. Get to know the owners of independent music labels that specialize in the kind of music you enjoy. All these people need help, generally.

Following this advice has opened several doors for me, including mastering the festival CD for the Charlotte Pop Festival for a few years. These opportunities may not have the financial backing to pay very well, if at all, but the rewards are indirect, and very real. Each band on the compilation now has a personal copy of your work, and if you perform well enough, they will seek you out for more work.

Having each band on a compilation go through the process to get a track mastered teaches them a repeatable skill; most people are creatures of habit and prefer to repeat something they already know how to do. It's great when money and work start flowing in without having to chase it down all the time.

Another thing that compilations (and especially tribute albums) are good for is to exercise your skills in making diverse tracks sound as though they all belong on the same album. For instance, I mastered the Buffalo Springfield tribute album *Five Way Street* for Not Lame Records in 2006. The incoming files were of all types, with broad variation not only in level (from too quiet to massively clipping) but also in studio technical skills. This disc turned out well, though, and I am proud of it, and working on it introduced me to 21 new potential clients!

Here are a couple of CD Architect screen shots that show the variation in the levels of artist submissions and how they looked after mastering. The first figure below is the "before" screen shot, showing the variety of submissions, and the second figure shows the CD as delivered, consistent across the board.

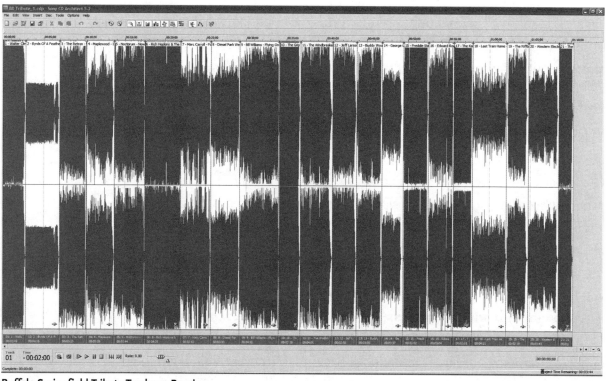

Buffalo Springfield Tribute Tracks as Receive

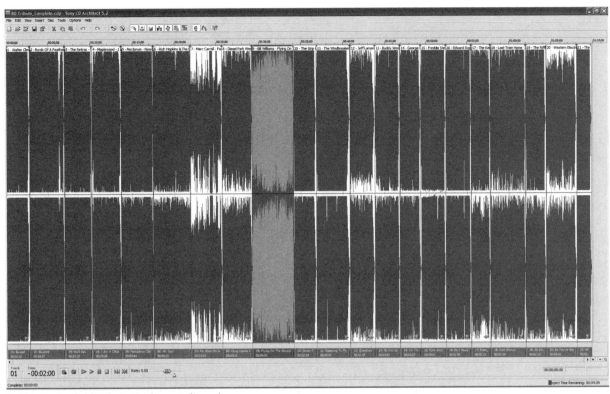

Buffalo Springfield Tribute Tracks as Delivered

Tribute Albums and Burning Sky Records

A steady stream of work arises from those with drive, and from our willingness to help them accomplish their goals. One of my favorite bands was Jellyfish, the members of whom I became friends with as a founder of a digital music distribution method (Weedshare 2002–2007). It turned out that there was a Jellyfish fan tribute album in the works by Alan Heaton. He had a MySpace page up for the project, and a few bands lined up. He originally found the bands through their live YouTube covers of Jellyfish songs.

Alan didn't have a lot of experience making records—he is a marketing manager at a pharmaceutical company. The MySpace page was a bit rough, and the tracks weren't sounding that good. What he did have was inspiration and drive; he intended to create a two-disc set composed of Jellyfish's two releases in their original order, plus extra unreleased material. I left some supportive comments on his MySpace page, and he wrote back on mine. We got in touch and I offered to master the tracks for the

Burning Sky Records Website

release. That led to some negotiations, but ended up with my not only mastering but also designing the art and co-producing the whole package.

There was a rich indie band presence in the heyday of MySpace, and finding participating bands worldwide for the tribute album was pretty easy for me because Alan was doing the legwork of band outreach and interfacing. This was also the peak time for CD Baby, and its charismatic founder, Derek Sivers. Derek was giving advice that bands should record cover versions for higher visibility in digital music stores when people search on songs they know. This worked out very well for us and our tribute albums.

In my mastering business, it has been helpful to work with bands from around the world through my work with Burning Sky Records. The bands are at all levels of proficiency, from bedroom studios to major-label artists working in professional studios. Each qualifying artist gets one free mastered track (that goes on the compilation). If the clients like what they hear, they'll come back for whole albums, and sequencing the tribute CDs is an additional benefit and joy for me.

Also, Alan and I both love the bands we are covering. In addition to Jellyfish, we have had a three-disc tribute to The Posies, a three-disc tribute to Roxy Music, and a track-for-track tribute of the first four Squeeze records. This becomes a triple value: having a driven partner (found on social networks) finding bands for you to master (from social networks) playing songs of bands you love.

Greatest Hits and Career Overview Box Sets

There are so many bands that try to make it, and so few that actually do—commercially at least. There is another type of success for bands, and that is to be influential. Many bands that never made it were the acts that your heroes went to see and were inspired by to play music or be "rock stars." I've had the opportunity to gather the work of some of these artists, and the restoration and compilation is a challenge due to the often-primitive recording conditions that bands just starting out employ.

This presents another opportunity to listen for work. Read interviews with your heroes (or ask them) about who their favorite artists were. There will be the standards, of course, but research the obscure bands. At some point, you may find a band that existed but none of their work was ever released, or that has an album on a major label but also a large back catalog of demos. These are great tasks to take on, primarily because musicians in forgotten bands may be grateful for your interest, and be willing to work with you on a remastering project.

Genealogy Transcriptions

Genealogy transcriptions are very interesting. Over the years I've had a few clients who have brought me old cassette tapes of their great-grandparents recalling stories of their lives and telling of their family tree. These can also be challenging.

The first one I worked on was recorded in the early 1970s on a portable cassette deck with a built-in microphone. The job was to clean up the audio enough to allow the client to transcribe the tape to a written story. The self-noise of the cassette tape motors on the recording obscured the voices of the interview, and I worked for hours trying to clean up the audio.

This recording, however, was beyond repair. But having listened to it so many times, I could make out what was being said. I learned to fail (sort of) fast, and went ahead and transcribed it myself, and returned that to the client. It was what he really wanted, and he was happy to pay for the work.

Forensics

Forensics is one of the most lucrative areas of audio restoration and, without exception, the most traumatic. I've had a couple of well-paying jobs from lawyers seeking to clarify and decode 911 tapes. I've found that this is not for me.

One instance was of a young father just after a car wreck that killed his family, and the other was a call from a pay phone just prior to a murder. The karma is very heavy, and if you are willing to trade it for high cash income, you may want to explore this field.

Companion CDs for Books and Instruction Manuals

I've mastered a companion CD for a graphic novel for Fantagraphic Books, and a companion CD for a couple of revisions of a guitar instructional book. These are somewhat unusual opportunities—but that is the point.

This gets back to listening for work. Both of these were referrals from existing clients (which is the best way to get work), but at the start of your career you may want to explore unusual paths.

Other Record Label Work

A record label (Chuckie-Boy Records) presented my first opportunity, and working with labels has proved to be a good idea from a business standpoint. One of the best aspects of working with a label is that it takes care of the more onerous tasks in the music industry: the legal and paperwork issues and artist relations.

One interesting job pointed out the benefits of being at the leading edge of technological transitions. An established indie label wanted to post MP3 versions of its tracks on its new website (when websites were new) and hired me to capture and convert their CD catalog to MP3 format files—just the way that every teenager has done these days since they were toddlers. At the time and with the technology available to us, this was actually a challenge. Stay tuned in to leading technological indicators, and get paid for what soon becomes commonplace. Don't get too attached to providing these kinds of services, and stay sensitive to when it is time to drop services that have become trivial and mundane. Always keep moving forward, and stay ahead of your clients technologically if you can.

Seattle Fireworks Audio

One of the best and most interesting opportunities that came across my desk was to provide the music assembly and final soundtrack editing for the Seattle Fourth of July fireworks display. One of my original mastering clients is the musical director for the company responsible for selecting and producing the music soundtrack to accompany the biggest fireworks display in Seattle. This turned out to be a great recurring job for me—I've done the fireworks audio soundtrack each year from 2006 through 2011.

When the client team first came to my studio in 2006, they brought an assortment of MP3s and a file of the previous year's program material to cut pieces from and drop into the current year's program. This was challenging from a mastering point of view because song-to-song consistency was totally missing and the music was spectrally all over the map. Here's an image of the files that were presented to me:

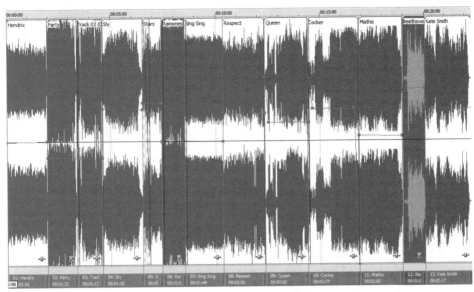

2006 (Before) CDA

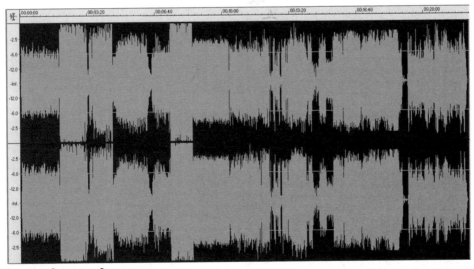

2006 (Before) Waveform

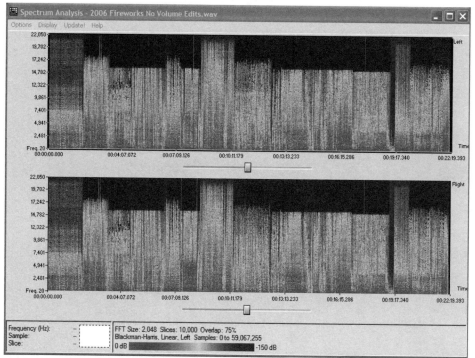

2006 (Before) Sonogram

This set did not allow for mastering, so we just had to adjust levels from track to track (and within tracks for fades). Then there was an Ultramaximizer in the master chain to control level excursions. You can still see the permanent damage in the sonogram from having compressed files that were sourced through iTunes or ripped lossily from a CD.

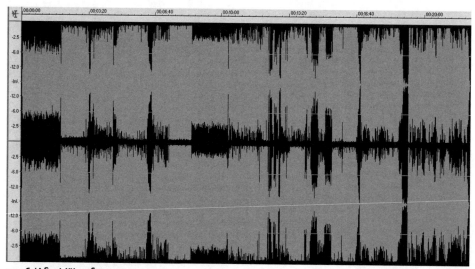

2006 (After) Waveform

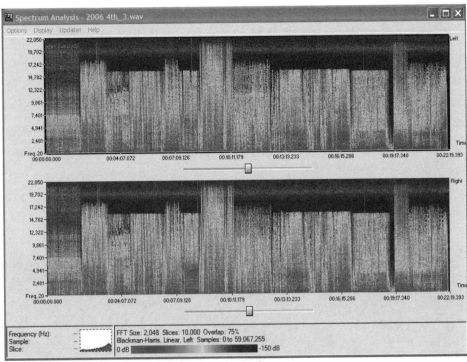

2006 (After) Sonogram Showing the Cloud of Noise Shaping

One challenge was what happened to the sound when the show was broadcast on radio and television. We attended the live fireworks display at Gasworks Park in Seattle on the Fourth, and the sound seemed acceptable there. We had a parking place on site that was close in, but when 30,000 people are walking out of the park on foot and you're in a car, it becomes pretty interesting. The solution was to drive at a walking pace—I'd never been in a motorcade before. We had recorded the broadcast on our DVR and when we made it home, we wanted to see how the show sounded.

We had stayed at home the year before to watch the show live on TV, and there had been a significant problem with the broadcast sound. As the show started, the music soundtrack volume was really soft; they were only broadcasting the sound coming over the public address system in the park. Halfway through the show, the broadcast audio was engaged and the sound came up to full volume.

So, we were interested in how the audio would sound this year, after having heard it earlier that night at the park. We cued it up on our new HDTV, but the broadcast sound was less than optimal. The problem was that not only were you hearing the audio being broadcast, but you were also hearing the explosions of the fireworks. There was a mic out there to pick up the explosions and crowd noises, and that was very near the P.A. system for 30,000 people. The live sound at the venue arrived a bit delayed to the broadcast audio and made for a challenging listen.

The figures below show the state of what was received in 2008, as mastered and unmastered files. Here you have all the songs I received in order, the way they came in. Note that they are all of different amplitudes. At the end of the process, there should be a smooth, flowing track order. Also note that these are the full songs as received in order, prior to edits and cutdowns.

The sonograms of these files are even more telling. Note that the majority of the tracks have no energy above 15 kHz or so, which is a sign of MP3 compression. The following figures show what was provided to me as the premaster files.

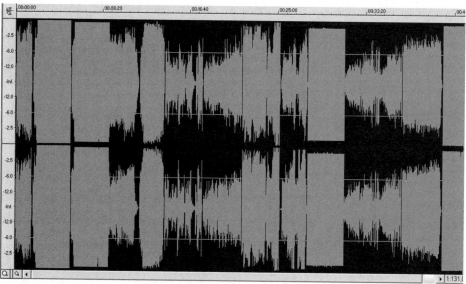

2008 (Before) Waveform

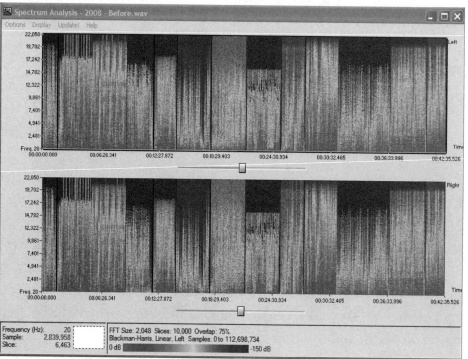

2008 (Before) Sonogram

The next two figures show the files as released.

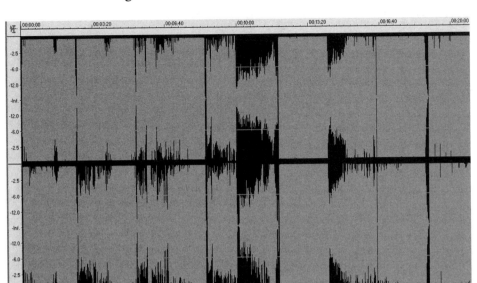

2008 (After) Waveform

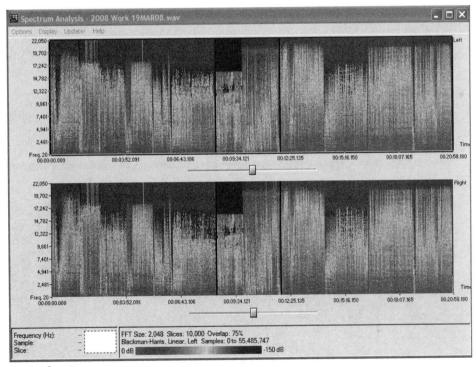

2008 (After) Sonogram

These are the mastered tracks as delivered. Note that they are now using the full resolution of the medium across the tracks. They may appear to be very compressed in this image, but they are not bad when zoomed out. How compressed a file looks visually can be affected by the length of the file; for example, a long file shown in a short window can appear loglike, even though it may just be the kick drum transients that are at full amplitude (as opposed to everything being at full amplitude).

In the sonogram view, notice how the high ends are extended as compared with the "before" image, and especially notice the "cloud" of noise shaping. One way you can tell if a file has been mastered through an Ultramaximizer with noise shaping on is that it takes all the broadband noise that is mathematically required because of DSP processing and "tilts it up" above 19 kHz. When you get a file in and you want to know where it has been and what has been done to it, if you see a cloud across the top as in the in the 2008 (After) Sonogram figure, that's the noise shaping you're seeing.

In later years, Chris Porter of One Reel took over the production reins, and we have used commercial CD releases as a beginning point for each show (as compared with multigeneration compressed MP3s as source audio). Even (and sometimes, especially!) the commercial CDs are harder to work with because of the Loudness Wars. It has regularly been the case that all I could do to a file was to reduce the level (from clipping) by −0.3 dB.

Fireworks Cutdowns

Each track for the fireworks show had to be *cut down* for length. This leads to some great waveform-editing practice. Here is a workflow:

1. Add markers to the tracks as they play through, denoting the major sections, as in the figure below.

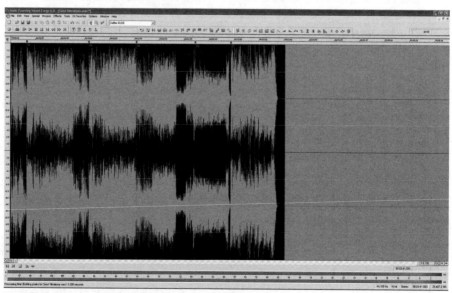

"Good Vibrations" with Markers on Major Sections

2. Skip from marker to marker to play back what should sound like the same parts in the song, like repeated choruses or the return from a guitar solo, as in the figure below.

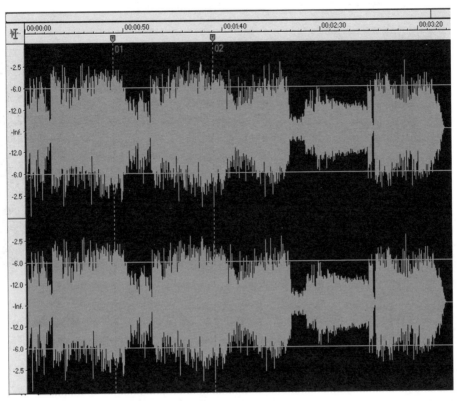

"Good Vibrations" with Markers to Jump Between

3. Zoom way in and move your marker at a sample-level resolution to find a first cut point that is as close to the zero-crossing in both channels as possible, as in the figure below.

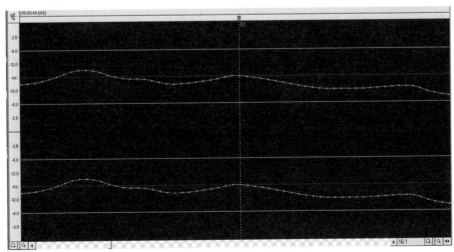

"Good Vibrations Edit," First Cut Point

4. Next, place another marker on a sample that leads into the same music later in the track with the same near zero-crossing low-level amplitude values. Pay close attention to the slopes of the waveform; they should match around the cut area, as in the figure below.

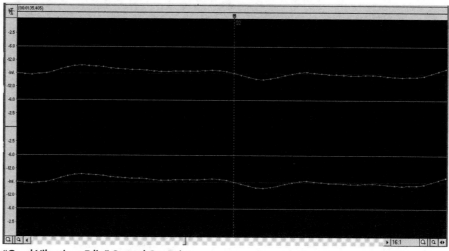

"Good Vibrations Edit," Second Cut Point

The intention here is to combine or juxtapose sounds so that they work together effectively. The key to this work is to respect the waveform direction and value; when this is done just right, it can be magical. Additional considerations have to be made based on instrumentation; often a track is built up more as it progresses, so listen for that in your practice.

Remember, this editing work is all about loudspeaker motion, and each sample you edit is actually a speaker-position indicator. If you can manage to fool the speaker into thinking there have been no changes to the smooth flow of the sample stream, the transition will be seamless.

The figure below shows the final cutdown of "Good Vibrations" for the fireworks show, and the QR code to the left of it leads to a video segment showing this work in action.

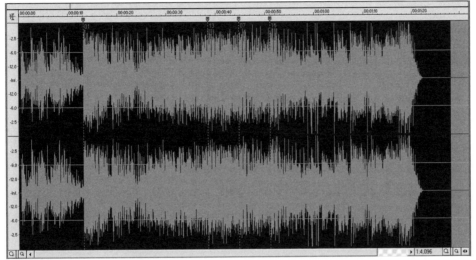

"Good Vibrations" Final Cutdown

Evening Magazine
Segment on the Fireworks Process

Your Client and Opportunity Bases Are Infinite

Hopefully, this chapter has shown the variety of opportunity available in the audio editing and mastering world. It is important to shift your attitude from looking for work to one of listening for how you can help others attain their goals—and offer that service.

Everywhere you go there are people asking for help. Qualify the opportunities where you can make a difference, and where your difference may earn compensation. Offer your services, but learn to fail fast, and keep listening.

Social networks are full of "We're just finishing up our album." That is an example of a flashing light for you to offer your assistance. The reason your clients and opportunities are infinite is that you can always find one more.

9

Mastering as a Business

Mastering your music is like mastering your life, and mastering your life includes mastering your productivity and your actions. The message to present to the world and to your clients with your life performance is "I am very busy, but highly efficient. Therefore I am available and can solve your issue, whatever it may be," as exemplified in the following quote:

> If you want a piece of work well and thoroughly done, pick a busy man. The man of leisure postpones and procrastinates, and is ever making preparations and 'getting things in shape'; but the ability to focus on a thing and do it is the talent of the man seeming o'erwhelmed with work.
>
> Elbert Hubbard, from *The Philosophy of Elbert Hubbard*
> (Wm. H. Wise & Co., 1930, page 42)

I've always considered successful retirement as when your vocation (what you do for work) and avocation (what you do for fun) are aligned. If you retire tomorrow and you happily keep on doing what you did today, then you are essentially already retired.

My passion was to retire into mastering, and I've been able to do that, among other pursuits. Here's the description of a day in my ideal mastering career: Wake up to finding 12 new tracks every morning to master in my dropbox, master them, get paid, and I'm done for the day. Lather, rinse, repeat.

There is a standard process called *the step function* that I address in each stage of my business life that guides what I offer. It looks like this: *take something > make it better > give it back > get paid*. In mastering, I don't have to compose or track or mix the album; I get to hear the finished

2-track, master it (make it better), return it, and get paid. I don't have to try to get it manufactured, and I don't have to try to sell or distribute it.

The same goes for my circuit board design work: I get a schematic (which I didn't have to design), lay out the Printed Circuit Board (make it better), return it, and get paid. I don't have to try to get it manufactured, and I don't have to try to sell it.

That being said, in all of these actions, the phrase *make it better* is key. Your results have to be of high quality, be manufacturable, and be saleable for you to stay in business. In this chapter I'll go over the techniques and processes that have worked for me over my past decade of self-employment.

The Business Bundle of Functionality

The beginning of any endeavor is challenging, since (by definition) one begins with nothing. If that is the case, let's shift our perspective: instead of considering this a beginning, let's gather everything you have ever done, all your skills and connections, and add them to today and call it a continuation. You are soaking in unrealized assets and your client base is infinite, since you can always add one more.

There are at least three things you need to acquire to launch your career: tools, skills, and clients. One of the most important tools to have at the beginning, and throughout your career, is information.

Begin Where You Are

It is a poor craftsman who blames his tools—a master can make beauty from anything. At the beginning of your mastering career, the clients and tools you'll start off with will not be in the million-dollar range. The improvements you'll provide are relative—I can make a broad range of musicians very happy at a reasonable rate; but I'd just as soon not work with someone who has already invested a huge amount in the studio. I'm happy to leave that work to the big rooms.

Learn to Fail Fast

Welcome all your professional challenges. Every problem you overcome is a problem that your competition will have to overcome as well, and you will gain additional "experience capital." If something isn't working out, try a different strategy. Begin again immediately after you fail. The faster you fail, the richer you get.

Determination is a driving force. There is also such a thing as "constructive failure," which occurs when you fail fast and begin again over and over until you succeed. Those people who point out failure in others are missing the opportunity to learn from their own failures and move forward. Failing is the raw material of success, and maintaining an internal belief in yourself trumps negative external input. When things do collapse (and they will), make note of what held fast and make use of those things in your further endeavors.

Generate and Cultivate a Brand

One of the most important tools at your disposal is fully under your own control: your brand. Make a logo, create a tagline, and get business cards. Promote your services whenever appropriate (but don't be an "energy vampire"). Have nice art and your logo on production master and listening copy CDs as in the figure to the left.

Remember that everything is a performance, and every online interaction is recorded forever. Have an Internet dropbox with your logo on it and a message to new (and existing) customers to make them feel welcome and informed as to the next steps in the process.

A Printed, Branded CD

Honor integrity in your brand and network with people of integrity; be part of an integrity chain. It's not who you know—it's who you are introduced by; so make connections only between people of integrity and that you trust.

Maintain nondisclosure. Don't share the work of others without explicit permission, or unless you've been asked to. Be a shock absorber, not an amplifier (avoid passing along gossip).

Maintain an awareness of your critical path—the set of actions that, if delayed, directly delay your delivery dates. Many items can be worked on at the same time, but there is only a single critical path to your goals. When you feel stuck about what your next step will be ask yourself, "What is the most important question?"—and answer that. Repeat.

The Business Card

A business card is another secret weapon in your business development arsenal. If your business card is eloquent, you don't have to be. Your business card is your first-line representation when meeting potential clients, and it stands in for you in your absence.

I have a special card, designed by Brad Marvin, called the MarCard (marketing card). This card opens up—twice! There is enough room to advertise the various services I offer and companies I am a part of, plus room for a bio and pictures. It really is a little resume/brochure.

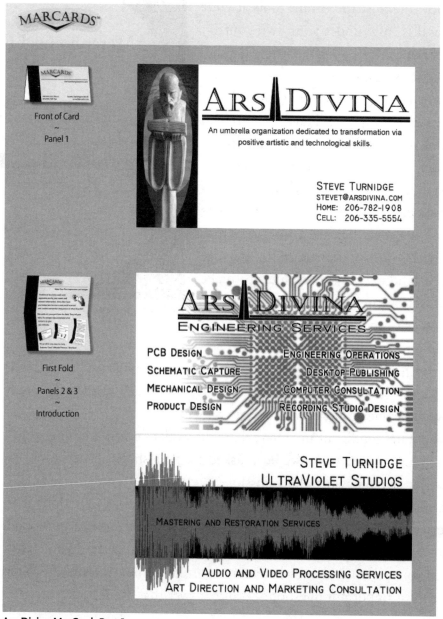

Ars Divina MarCard, Part 1

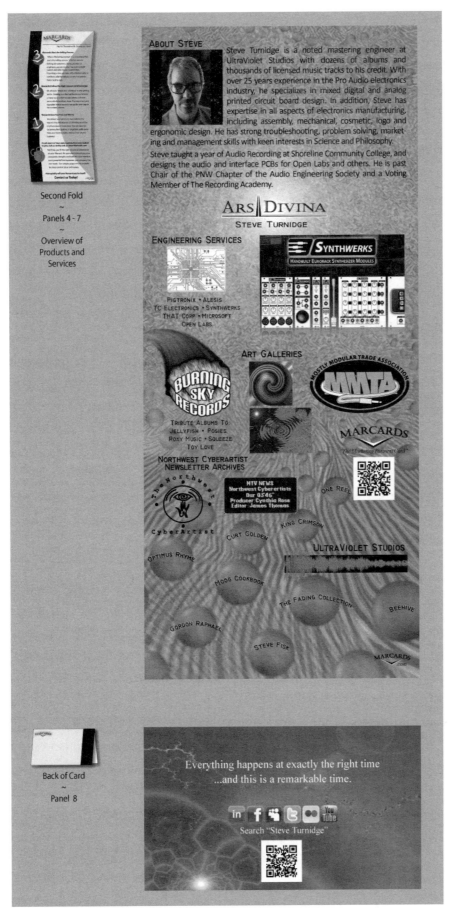

Second Fold
~
Panels 4 - 7
~
Overview of
Products and
Services

Back of Card
~
Panel 8

Ars Divina MarCard, Part 2

Another advantage a MarCard has over flat business cards is how it is received in a group. It can be a little rude, but it does sell itself—I don't have to push too hard. In a group, my card is typically the one that gets the most attention, and that gives me a competitive advantage. It is shown in the two figures following.

The Business Card Binder

Have and maintain a three-ring binder with business card binder pages to store your harvested business cards. Take your business card binder to networking events and conferences (you may want to have just a few pages in a smaller binder for travel). Load up a few pages with your own cards; then, as you collect cards, replace your cards with theirs. This arranges your business card/contact binder by event, time, and context.

The Ars Divina MarCard Website

Use QR Codes (or their current equivalent)

You'll notice two square bar codes on my business card. These are Quick Response (QR) codes and can be read by smartphones and tablets (as you have seen and experienced throughout this book). In the case of my card, the inside QR code, the first one show to the left, leads to a fully linked version of the card on a website. This website clearly connects to all my social media and many of my clients.

Digital Music News

The other QR code is a Google vanity search on "Steve Turnidge," which generates a biographical link list that I don't have to actively keep up to date (but could be challenging for the infamous).

Stay Informed

Stay current with news in the music and computing business. This information "currency" can be thought of as legitimate legal tender; it is your earned stock in trade. You can apply it to your career and, if successful, become a consultant. All you have to be is more informed than the client, and provide a genuine service.

The Pho Mailing List

Read mailing lists daily. Subscribe to Digital Music News (second QR code on left) and to the Pho list (third QR code on left). I also enjoy reading Science Daily (fourth QR code on left) to gain better perspective about the future. I read each of these on my phone before getting out of bed in the morning (one of the benefits of rock-star hours).

Another benefit of being on professional mailing lists and participating on professional forums is discovering information about the ideas of

Science Daily

influential people and the way they manage their relationships to one another. These are people who get things done, and they can be taken as role models—both positive and negative.

To be heard, speak into the microphone, not into the loudspeaker (even though that is where the loud sounds seem to be coming from). Instead of talking to the newspapers, talk to the newsmakers.

Starting a Business

Before starting a business, first be confident that you are good enough at what you do to provide an adequate value for the price you'll charge. When you think you are ready to have a go at any type of business, get a business license—that lets you legally receive money for your work. This is a good thing, and easier to do than you may think.

In addition, register your trade name(s) with the state, and reinforce your brand. In my home state (Washington), you can register whatever trade name you wish, even if someone else has registered it already. But the legal owner is the one who does business on the account first.

This is a good way to start up a brand: get a bank account in your trade name and start doing business on it right away. My bank had to see the state-issued business license with the trade name listed before opening the account. Make sure you document this. For instance, try to get paid with a check written out to your trade name and deposit it in your account, and make sure to keep a copy of the check and the dated deposit slip. This sets your start time in your business under that name in case there is a dispute (and hopefully you get there first).

Business Insurance

Get business insurance. Home insurance usually does not cover businesses in the home; if, for example, someone trips and falls leaving your house on a business visit, it is likely not covered. At the very least, look into the matter and read your insurance policy.

Another form of insurance is to report your income and pay your taxes. It is unwise to underreport cash transactions, and it can become a limiting factor for your business growth. At some point, make a decision to start your business and to follow the rules; then you'll be ready for success. A shady operation has more stress overhead than is healthy for you.

Mileage and Travel

Record your mileage for tax purposes, and note qualifying trips by maintaining a mileage book. A good way to do this is to have a little notebook and pen handy in the glove compartment or door of your car. Each time you leave home, write the current mileage, destination, and date on a line. If it is a trip for business, write a little (m) beside the destination. When tax time comes around, this provides a great way to total up your business mileage for the year.

Only starting mileages need to be recorded, since trip length can be calculated between consecutive entries.

Keep a Lab Notebook

This tip is one of the most important ones in this book and has been my key to keeping things straight in my business for a decade. Number each page of your notebook in the lower corners of the pages, starting at page 1, and carry the numbering on to your next notebook. Write the date in your lab notebook every day, and write the day at the first entry of each new page.

Your lab notebook documents your work life and can be used as proof of prior art to ensure your inventions and business dates of first creation. It is important that it is not a loose-leaf binder—that can invalidate date claims.

Take notes about your work, record phone numbers, and write to-do lists. Draw little squares in front of each to-do item in your lab notebook, and check the squares off when each item is complete. This provides an easy way to scan the pages of your notebook for unchecked to-do item squares.

Buy Post-it flags and mark important items (user names, account numbers) as they are recorded in your lab notebooks. Record transaction information in your lab notebook; put a dollar sign over the page number of your lab notebook if that page records income or expense.

When you do get paid, receive it in your lab notebook and record it in a receipt book that office supply stores carry. This gives you a written record of your earnings, and you can give duplicate receipts to your clients. Write your lab notebook page number on each receipt and other various types of paperwork.

Keep a three-ring receipt binder (to store receipts of purchased items, bank deposits, and other dated documents). Use 12 sheet protectors (one for each month) in your receipt binder and write the month in permanent marker on each sheet protector spine and make a new binder each year. This becomes very helpful at tax time.

Money

Value your time at a specific monetary personal hourly rate. If you charge clients less than your personal rate, you are subsidizing the client. You are paying yourself your personal rate when you watch TV or play video-games. This is especially important if you are freshly self-employed: take that extra 40 to 80 hours a week that you would have been working hard for someone else, and work hard for yourself. If what you are doing is truly your heart's desire, it won't seem like work at all.

Setting a low, reasonable compensation rate for your work ensures a steady stream of young and first-time clients. These, over time, become older repeat clients, who provide the best word-of-mouth marketing to diverse circles of their friends.

My rates (at this writing) are $50 per mastered track (payable via PayPal), which at the beginning of my career used to be $50 per hour when each track took four hours. Now that the desktop mastering chain is in place, and $50 per track is a realistic transaction and is close to the value I place on my time—plus, I am being paid for doing my heart's desire!

Invoicing

Invoicing is a great way to be paid. When I first started working for myself, I was very shy about asking for money. One of the first independent paying jobs I had was to write an article on the Sonic Foundry Noise Reduction plug-in for *EQ* magazine in 1999. We agreed on $200 for the article. I waited months and months to be paid, assuming that they knew what was going on, but I was in the wrong—I had never sent them an invoice for the project. When dealing with businesses with accounting departments, they need the full paper trail to generate payment. I let it go for a couple of years, until I hit "golden poverty" and had to look around for any "low hanging fruit" income opportunities. I wrote up an invoice and sent it to the company, and within a week I was paid.

The Client Environment

Make sure your studio is a friendly place that your clients look forward to visiting. Keep in mind that this is often their last step on a very long journey—they actually get their CD from you!

Comfortable seating behind your workstation is good, and having a client monitor is very important because it lets them follow along with what is happening. During sequencing and the "snap game," I typically ask them to shut their eyes, so they aren't influenced by where the tracks are (as compared to where they should be).

One thing that works is to always have a bowl of fresh candies available in the hallway on the way in and out, which leaves a sweet taste in their mouth when they think back on their time working with you in your studio.

Client Contact and Recruitment

Audio Engineering Society

Clients can be found in a number of ways. The key is to listen for work, not look for work. Don't be shy; make yourself known. Use inanimate agents such as business cards to promote your work for you when you're not around.

Be a shining light in your community—join the local audio and production associations and societies: the Audio Engineering Society (top left QR code) and the Producers and Engineers Wing of the Recording Academy (bottom left QR code) provide great opportunities to interact with people that can use your help. If these societies don't exist in your area, contact them to set up a section or chapter in your town, or travel to their events in other regions. This expands your potential client base beyond the local area.

Producers and Engineers Wing of the Recording Academy

Client Communications

Use Skype or other telepresence tools—they are the windows in the cubicle wall to your global client base. I have clients around the world that I work with as easily as if they were in my room. I can share my screen, or even aim the webcam at my screen and point and measure with my hands onscreen (this is really helpful when laying out circuit boards). A good Skype tip is to make an interesting backdrop—something as simple as a nice tapestry hung over a clothesline behind you can do wonders for your image.

Marketing Methods

The global marketplace has a seemingly infinite number of clients (you can always add one). Just as sound is always around you, opportunities surround you as well. Be close and responsive to the phone and email, and every time the phone rings, it could be a client or potential client—and answer it accordingly.

Even telemarketers may need some tracks mastered. I do audio consulting work for my mail carrier, who reached out to me because of the music magazines that came in my mail, but it goes to show that you are surrounded by unrealized assets. Every conversation you have holds a seed of potential work to be planted and tended and to grow at agricultural time frames. Keep your phone's outgoing message short and concise— respect your clients' time.

Also, stay on the lookout for business opportunities for your friends, and provide them if you can. In the same way, find opportunities to pay for the work of others, then you are more likely to get paid. Be a part of a lucrative networking ecosystem.

The Four-Foot Forks

There was a story I was told as a child regarding sharing, but is directly applicable to word-of-mouth networking and referrals. In this story, a person dies and is offered the choice of going to heaven or to hell. The deceased asks to see each first, in order to make an informed decision. The tour starts in hell, where a grand table is laid out with excellent food, but the guests at the table are gaunt and haggard. On closer observation, it is noticed that instead of arms, all the table guests have four-foot forks and find it impossible to feed themselves, and are therefore starving.

The tour then continues in heaven, where surprisingly enough the same tableau is set up, except in this instance, everyone is happy, healthy, and well fed, even with the four-foot forks as arms. The main difference is that at this table, each person is feeding the person across from them.

Competition is fine, but co-opetition is better. Help as many people find work as you can, and the example and appreciation should flow your way.

The Talent Tarot

One set of cards to collect personally is business cards, but there is an organization and facilitation thought experiment to organize your connections: the "talent tarot." Take everyone you know and (mentally) place them each on a separate card. List their strengths and desires. This is the beginning of your personal talent tarot—the deck you shuffle through to find bandmates, references, or collaborators.

There are a couple of sets in this deck: the major and minor arcana. The minor arcana of the talent tarot are people who are very public and accessible—almost anyone has access to them.

The major arcana are those highly skilled individuals that shun social networking; you have to actually know them to make introductions or ask for collaboration. These are very valuable connections, usually made only in person.

Making and collecting these connections is a great reason to attend local and national audio networking events like AES (Audio Engineering Society) and NARAS (National Academy of Recording Arts And Sciences—the Grammy Award people) meetings and conventions. The great thing is that they collect you in their talent tarot as well!

Self-Employment

If you find yourself freshly self-employed, one of the best things you can do for your state of mind (and your future) is to stay as busy and productive as possible. What to do? Do what you love and love to do. If you have a particular favorite aspect of your life (music, art, programming, flower arranging, it could be anything), dive into it. If it requires capital, dive into the communities that focus on the activities. If you can't find a community that centers around your special interest, form one.

Remember, you now have 40 hours returned to you for your use each week, so keep them productive. If you are visibly productive, it will be noticed by your community of personal clients—and there are always people who need something done. If they are wise and follow the idea behind the quote that opened this chapter, you may be the busy person called on to perform.

If you are self-employed, you may have the option to go into golden poverty. If you do reach this state, be close and responsive to the phone and e-mail. Stay aware of opportunities around you—social networks are the watercoolers of the self-employed.

In deciding what to do, always remember that the universe makes the setlist. Don't look for work—listen for work.

The Social Graph

In social networking (a key to succeeding in the mastering (or any) business), the bundle of functionality is a set of social networks taken together to generate a "social graph."

An autograph, or signature, on a contract or document stands in for you when you are not there. It defines you in the real world: if you sign a check, your autograph ensures that you actually made the decision and agreement to pay money to someone or some entity.

A similar concept can be extended into the social media arena regarding your social graph. Your social graph is what you post, who your friends are, who your top friends are, your status messages, and the way you present yourself online.

It is what defines you in the online world. It is your higher-dimensional cross-section (including the passage of time) in the social universe. An autograph happens once; a social graph accretes and aggregates all of your behaviors. It truly is a performance that defines you. It is critically important to present your performance consciously; for example, you probably wouldn't get up onstage in front of 2,000 people and tell them how hungover you are, or what a bad day you are having.

Use Social Networks as Performance Spaces

- LinkedIn is backstage. It is for VIPs and important business connections only.
- Facebook is the stage. It is where you live out your life with people you like.
- MySpace (used to be) the audience. It (was) where you take all comers and broadcast your work (the Burning Sky Records tribute album projects were mostly populated by bands we met on MySpace).
- Twitter is telepathy training. It enables you to know the state of a person at a distance—right now.

Life Streaming

The act of generating status messages and a social graph is called "life streaming"; you "life stream to your social graph." Personally, I focus on Facebook and post many scientific articles and audio-technology links. I actually consider my profession to be posting links on Facebook. I get the benefit of reading the articles, and those who are connected to me get the benefit of my research and information discoveries as an added value. As people become used to reading interesting things I have posted, this gives me the chance to post items about my services. The posting ratio feels like 99 useful links to each self-serving link. I guess you could call it the new form of marketing—the "hot apple pie on the windowsill" version of marketing.

Instead of taking the pie, cutting it up, wrapping it in plastic, going to the market and yelling "Get your apple pie here!" you place the hot fragrant apple pie on the windowsill and let people be attracted to the scent. If you can get your work out passively, you can stimulate interest from your client base.

Status Messages

Status messages are very important because of the associative property. When I post a status that says "Steve is mastering" or "Steve is doing printed circuit board design," this informs the readership who may be in need of mastering or PCB design that I am a source for those functions.

It used to be that everyone could be famous for 15 minutes; now we are famous for the 15 seconds someone spends reading our status message. Hopefully you are famous for the 15 seconds in which someone is making a decision on who to hire. Generating useful status messages often keeps your services at top of mind in your client base (and potential client bases).

Be Everywhere at Once

One key to being everywhere at once is to have a master collateral store of your bio, pictures, and metadata-style information—that is, everything that you need to set up an account or a page at any given social networking site. Think of each site as a copy of your "book," placed where people congregate. In this way you can be everywhere all the time. Your master collateral store can also be your personal webpage.

Also, there are secret weapons. Hellotxt.com is one of these (see QR code on right). Status messages entered here propagate to all your social sites that provide status updates. In this way, a generally static page at one of your many points of presence can appear to be regularly updated, and you can create the generally unchanging static pages from your master collateral store.

Hellotxt.com

People hang out at places they are comfortable with. For example, business people hang out on LinkedIn, others prefer Facebook, and others may prefer MySpace or a different social network. Hellotxt provides a way of being everywhere all at once and messaging people where they naturally live.

Utilize the constellation of social networks. Find out where your clients hang out and create a presence there. For that matter, create a presence on as many sites as you are comfortable with maintaining.

Use Social Networks at Their "Sharp End"

Setting up the sites is just the beginning. Make sure that you have the sites set to email you the comments made on your page so you can monitor them. The next key is to use each service at its "sharp end" (like a pencil). For instance, LinkedIn is great for business relationships—only connect to those you would like to have refer you or that you would refer. Facebook is the stage your life is played out on; connect here with those you wish to have and interact with in your life. In addition, create a Facebook Artist page for your general public interactions.

MySpace used to be a good place to reach out to a broad, generally younger audience. Take all comers and monitor comments for spam. The loss of MySpace popularity is a drag. It was excellent to connect with and acquire new bands for Burning Sky Records, but when it staled out, no clear replacement in the bundle of functionality has risen to take its place—yet.

Comments Are Currency

Each time someone "likes" a post you've put up on Facebook, you learn a couple of things: first, you find out that at least someone is reading your posts, and second, you learn another bit about what that someone enjoys. Each "like" is another 15 seconds of fame, and those tend to add up.

There is another great way to interact with your clients and potential clients: write recommendations for people on LinkedIn or other sites that allow recommendations. It only takes a few minutes and spreads lots of goodwill; it's today's version of a thank-you letter. Try to connect with your audience—I mean your clients—wherever they like to hang out. The more you know about them, the more you are "listening for work."

With all these sites, use the concept of leverage and fulcrums. If you are doing everything yourself manually, it is as if the fulcrum is very close to you, and you have to expend a lot of energy to lift a load. Using tools that multiply your leverage is like moving the fulcrum far away, giving you much more action with much less time and energy expended.

Planning Ahead and Goal Setting

If you actually achieve your five-year goal, you've aimed too low. A good exercise is to consider where you want to be in five years. Your goal can be based only on what you know right now, so it will be pretty shady. Picture yourself achieving the advanced station of your five-year goal, and then consider where you have to be to achieve that goal.

Next, take the "one-step removed" goal, and think again about where you'd need to be to achieve *that* goal. Repeat this process until you are exactly one step away from the present—the beginning point of the chain of goals.

Now, wipe them all out and focus directly on that very next step that leads to the five-year goal. When you achieve that goal, repeat the process from your more experienced vantage point, and keep tuning in on the intersection of what you really want and what is actually possible.

10

Fundamentals of Audio

When you listen to music, live or at home, sound waves are propagated in the air where they are affected by materials in the environment on the way to impacting your hearing systems. This overview of the physicality of sound should provide a bit of a foundation to add to and integrate with your understanding of the process of desktop mastering.

The Ocean of Air

When we discuss the concept of audio, we are talking about air—the atmosphere, to be precise, and vibrations in the atmosphere. What is considered to be standard air pressure in the room is actually very high pressure at the bottom of an ocean of air. At sea level, it is approximately 14.7 pounds per square inch, or 1 kilogram per square centimeter. Air pressure, in this case, is measured by a barometer. Sound pressure, on the other hand, is a (usually) small variation in air pressure, which is measured not with a barometer, but with a sound-pressure-level meter.

Air, while seeming so transparent and, well, "airy" most of the time, actually has mass and elasticity. You see the mass of air when the wind blows in the trees, and you experience the elasticity of air in tires and bicycle pumps: when you press on air it gets smaller. Air also expands back when it can, as in a toy balloon.

When you push on air, it gets smaller; it compresses and becomes denser. When you let go of the air, it expands, or *rarifies*, becoming less dense. This is what happens at the surface of your loudspeaker: when the speaker cone moves out the air compresses, generating a positive pressure above the air pressure in the room. When the speaker cone moves in, it creates a suction or negative pressure, and the air rarifies. In between those two states, the pressure at the speaker neutralizes to the air pressure in the room again. This oscillating, undulating wave of sound pressure is called (not surprisingly) a *waveform*.

If the sound pressure were local to only the speaker surface, we wouldn't hear anything at a distance from the speaker. There is a physical phenomenon called *wave propagation* that takes care of delivering the sound to our ears.

Propagation

Consider the air, which has mass and elasticity, to appear in one dimension as a series of weights (the mass) chained together with springs (the elasticity). If you impact the first weight in the chain, it will compress the spring it is attached to and push that spring into the next weight in line, which then compresses its spring in turn. The first weight, after it has delivered the energy to the next one, wants to return to a resting state, which stretches the spring out until it also returns to a resting state where they all began. Meanwhile, the impact is propagated down the chain of weights until the friction in the system causes the force of the impact to dissipate, as shown in the figure to the left.

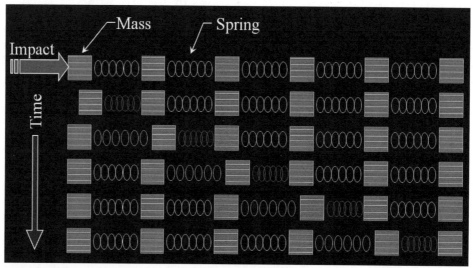

A one-dimensional representation of wave motion in a medium

Note that the first weight that was hit did not travel down the chain to the end. It imparted its energy to the next weight, and so on. It was the energy that traveled through the system.

The chain of weights and springs described above works fine for a straight line, but let's add a dimension. Wave motion in water coming from a pebble dropped in a pond travels across a plane in two dimensions over the surface of the pond in all directions. The water compresses up into a wave and falls back into a trough. We again find a waveform as seen in following two figures.

Waves in Water

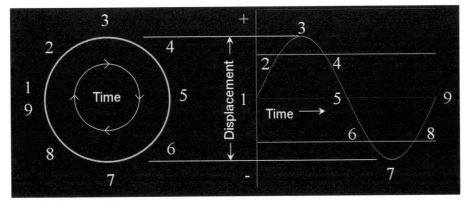

Waves in Water over Time

**Longitudinal and
Transverse Wave Motion**

One interesting fact: as a wave travels through the water, individual particles travel in clockwise circles! The radius of the circles decrease as the depth of the water increases (see QR code to the left).

When we take propagation into the third dimension, we find three-dimensional expanding shells of compression. If you light a firecracker, for instance, you will get a wave front of compressed air pushing molecules longitudinally in all directions away from the source of the sound. Those molecules impart the force to the next shell of molecules, and so on. A steadily vibrating object sends out a series of shells of compression.

A string under tension, such as a guitar string, that is attached to a resonating object, like a guitar, vibrates back and forth when plucked, transferring its energy into the body of the guitar. The string vibrates up and down, sideways, or transversely to the direction of the sound coming from the soundboard of the guitar (see figure below).

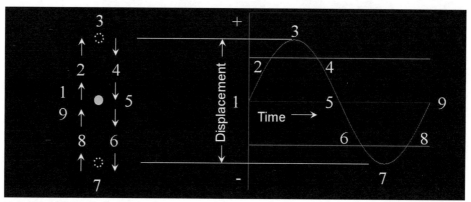

Transverse Motion in Strings

An interesting fact about plucked strings is that the actual shape of the string at any moment is a straight line sharply bent at one point. It is the bend, or kink, that travels from end to end of the string at the vibrating frequency of the note (see figure below).

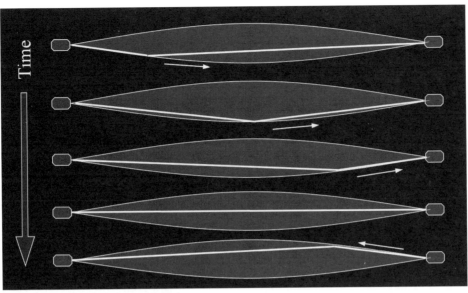

Transverse Motion in Strings with Kink

The Waveform Explained

I often give my clients an audio refresher at the beginning of our sessions, because it helps us get on the same page and gets them thinking in the right direction.

We start with a picture of a sine wave in a digital audio workstation, as is shown below. This is a typical waveform, like one you would see in Sony Creative Software Sound Forge, for instance. The straight line down the middle of the waveform is the atmospheric pressure in the room, the speaker at rest—silence. During silence, no sound is produced from the speaker (this is also known as black noise).

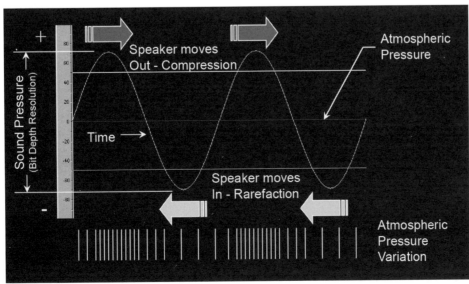

The Sine Wave

When the sine wave, which is the audio signal, goes above the straight line, the pressure rises in the room, and the speaker moves out; when the waveform goes below the straight line, the speaker moves in, rarefying the air in the room. So as the waveform travels along in time, you are actually seeing a direct analog (crossovers notwithstanding) of what the speaker is doing at the speaker cone. If the waveform follows the straight line, there is no sound. As you see the waveform travel by on the computer screen, that is a dynamic vision of a speaker going in and out.

Low frequencies are the large occasional swings, and high frequencies ride on the low frequencies. It is useful to visualize the frequency content of a waveform that is playing and speeding by on the screen. I typically like to watch the motion at a waveform zoom level of 16:1. The sample files on the DVD-ROM include videos of premastered and mastered files playing at this zoom level.

As the waveform goes by, you can see bright areas that are the high frequencies, and more open areas that are the low frequencies. Eventually, you can calibrate your eye to see when something is too sibilant by the brightness of the waveform.

In the waveform view you are seeing the full bandwidth of the audio. When this signal gets to your speaker, the crossover takes the low frequencies and routes them to the woofers, and the high frequencies (that ride on the low frequencies) are sent to the tweeters.

For instance, the first figure following shows a 1 kHz sine wave. This will be mixed with the 60 Hz sine wave seen in the second figure. In the third figure, you see what is happening at the speaker: the high frequencies are riding on the low frequencies.

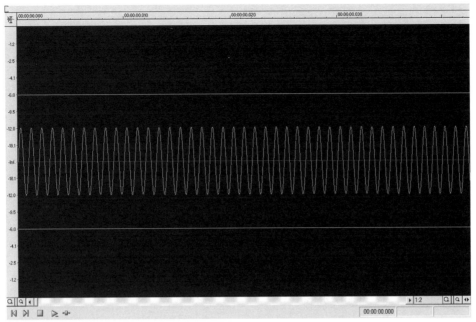

A 1 kHz Sine Wave

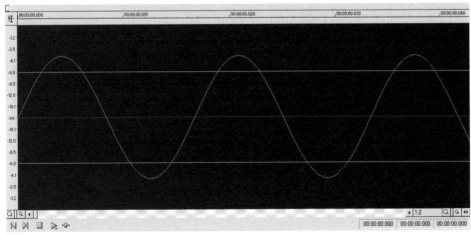

A 60 Hz Sine Wave

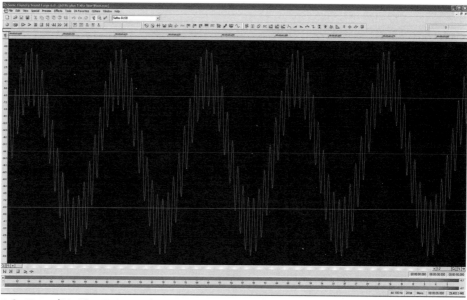

A 60 Hz + 1 kHz Sine Wave Result

Units of Measurement: the Decibel (dB)

The story of the decibel begins in the early days of telephony, when engineers sought a way to measure changes *in* things, rather than the things themselves. For instance, how much would a signal drop in level over a one-mile distance of telephone wire? They chose to call this measurement the *Bel* in honor of Alexander Graham Bell, inventor of the telephone. The Bel turned out to be quite an unwieldy measurement for smaller ratios, so in 1928 the Bell (telephone) System chose to decimate it (divide by ten) and call it the *decibel*—hence, 10 decibels = 1 Bel.

Being a ratio, decibels have no units in themselves; they are always used in comparison to other things. Decibels can measure the ratios between power gains—like sound-pressure level (SPL), which starts with 0 dB being the threshold of hearing and 120 dB being the threshold of pain. The decibel can also be the ratio between power losses, like dBFS, which starts with 0 dBFS (a digital audio reference level equal to "Full Scale") as the highest value, and counts down from there using negative numbers.

Everything Is Relative

Any given measurement expressed in decibels is relative to the 0 dB reference value. This is always used as one of the numbers for the ratio—even if 0 dB means different things, which it does when used to describe different measurements.

Another interesting aspect of decibels is that they are logarithmic, or nonlinear. From 0 dB to 120 dB (the threshold of pain) to be counted out in linear numbers is to count from 1 to 1,000,000.

There is an interesting challenge with measuring levels, especially averaging levels. If you took only the mean (average) of a sine wave, the result would usually be zero; this is because the wave goes above and below zero by the same amount in each cycle. The solution to this problem is to use a measurement called root-mean-square (RMS), which is the square root of the mean (average) of the sum of the squares of each point on the waveform. RMS guarantees results that are always positive because a square of either a positive or a negative number always results in a positive number.

Here are some of the flavors of decibels and their references:

- 0 dB SPL is the threshold of hearing, measuring sound pressure.
- 0 dBu is 0.775 Vrms, measuring voltage. Balanced (professional) gear references +4 dBu to 1.23 Vrms.
- 0 dBm is 1 milliwatt, measuring current (power), particularly line-level signals. The value of dBm (or the power ratio in decibels [dB] of the measured power referenced to one milliwatt [mW]) is also what VU (volume unit) meters are calibrated to, measuring average peaks. 0 VU = +4 dBm on balanced gear, and 0 VU = –10 dBm on unbalanced gear.

Characteristics of a Wave

Join me for a tour of the seven characteristics of a wave.

Amplitude—This term generally corresponds to loudness or level. There are different ways of measuring amplitude. Peak level measures from a zero-crossing to the maximum positive or maximum negative excursion of the wave. Peak-to-peak level is measured from maximum positive to maximum negative amplitude of the wave. Loudness is generally measured with RMS values.

Frequency—This refers to how often something happens. A waveform frequency measures how often a complete occurrence of the waveform repeats. We are most familiar with *frequency* being referred to as a measurement of pitch in sound; for instance, a waveform that cycles at 440 times in a second is known as the note A4 (middle A) on a piano. Frequency is measured in cps (cycles per second) or Hertz (Hz), over 999 referred to as 1 kHz (kilohertz).

Velocity—This is the speed at which a waveform propagates through a given medium. The speed of sound at 70° F in air: 1,128 feet per second, 344 meters per second, or 769 miles per hour. This speed is affected by the medium and temperature, and not by the frequency or amplitude of a wave.

Knowing the speed of sound is convenient when figuring out the delay of a distant event, like lightning. Since a mile is 5,280 feet, and the speed of sound is 1,128 feet per second, then sound travels roughly a mile in 5 seconds. Turned around, sound travels roughly 1 foot per millisecond, so if you are 100 feet away from a stage, the time between seeing an event and hearing it would be a tenth of a second. This has nothing to do with the speed of electricity in wires, which travels at or near the speed of light.

Wavelength—This is the distance between the beginning and end of a cycle, in an environment in which the wave propagates. It is a measurement of length of a single cycle, which is good to know when you have a given frequency building up in your room.

Phase—This is a relationship between two similar waveforms that are offset from one another in time. Phase is measured in degrees. *Complete cancellation* is 180°, *perfect phase* is 0°. *Phase shift* describes amount of lead or lag from one wave to another.

Harmonic Content—This is what gives sound its taste (in audio, also known as *timbre*). Just as with juice mixes—either it is a straight single-fruit juice, or it can be a rich blend of many different flavors. The equivalent of a single-juice drink in waveforms is the sine wave, which is called a *simple* waveform. Square, triangle, and sawtooth are *complex periodic* waveforms, which are continuous and repetitive (vowels in speech are made of these).

Complex waveforms are made up of multiple sine waves added together, and that is one of the underpinning concepts in digital audio—that any complex waveform can be created by adding sine waves of different frequencies and amplitudes together.

The father of this concept was a French mathematical physicist named Joseph Fourier (1768–1830), who developed the Fourier transform, which states: "Any periodic vibration, however complicated, can be built up from a series of simple vibrations, whose frequencies are harmonics of a fundamental frequency, by choosing the proper amplitudes and phases of these harmonics."

Fourier studied how heat flows through an object when it is heated up, finding that the movement of heat also behaves like a wave. This was the beginning of the breakthrough discovery that all complex waves are made up of various simple sine waves added together.

Back to the juice analogy: Let's say that the fundamental frequency (sound that corresponds to the note being played; for example, the first harmonic) is apple juice—(the sine wave)—it is a pure and simple tone. If you add other flavors (the harmonics) to the juice, it starts to become something else altogether. These flavors are always related to the fundamental frequency mathematically, as multiples of the fundamental for periodic waveforms.

Even harmonics (two, four, and six times the frequency when added together with the fundamental) are thought to be smooth and warm and work well with the fundamental. These are *consonant harmonics*. Odd harmonics (three and five times the fundamental) are *dissonant harmonics* and have a more closed, covered effect. So, we mix up the juices of the fundamental and its harmonics, and we get complex waveforms.

If you are trying to find out what fruits are in a blended juice drink, reading the list of ingredients gives a lot of information. There is a tool that can analyze your complex waveform and present a list of simple frequencies and their amplitudes (the ingredients). This is called a Fast Fourier Transform (or FFT for short). This list is usually presented on a graph, and as such it is the waveform transformed into a visual representation.

The coolest thing about this discovery is that you can learn what frequencies combine to make the other simple waveforms. My favorite, and the most informative, is the square wave. Square waves are of special interest in the mastering field, because clipped waveforms square up. Knowing what makes the sharp corners gives yet another reason to avoid clipping. The figure below shows a 1 kHz square wave.

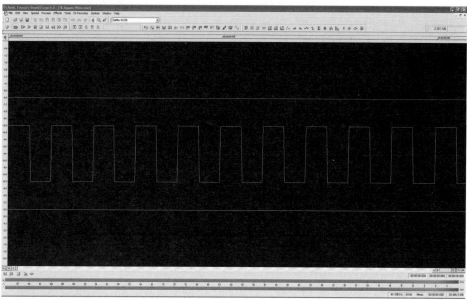

A 1 kHz Square Wave

Remember that odd harmonics are usually musically dissonant? Well, a square wave is chock full of odd harmonics. A 1 kHz sine wave, for instance, has a single harmonic component, naturally, at 1 kHz, as shown in an FFT (Fast Fourier Transform) display in the first figure to the right. To create a square wave out of sine waves, take that fundamental and add odd harmonics of an increasingly lower amplitude as such: one-third times the third harmonic, one-fifth times the fifth harmonic, one-seventh the seventh harmonic and so on. This is graphically displayed in the second figure to the right in an FFT image of a 1 kHz square wave. The interesting thing about a square wave is that higher frequencies "square up" the corners.

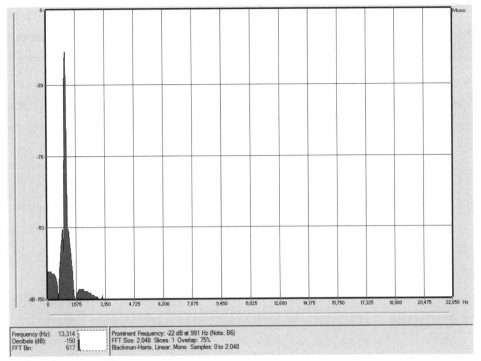

A 1 kHz Sine Wave FFT

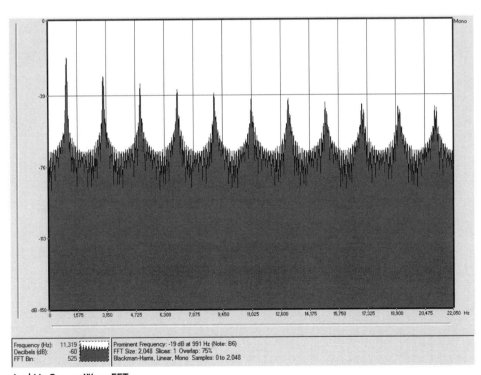

A 1 kHz Square Wave FFT

In audio test equipment, a 1 kHz square wave is used as a waveform to test frequency range. If the corners of the square wave come out rounded, then the test reveals a limited high-frequency response. Likewise, clipped waveforms, or clipping in speakers, generate a significant amount of odd harmonics. In the worst cases this can cause destruction of the playback chain, the speakers and amplifiers. Pay close attention to this and try to avoid unintentional clipping.

The Envelope—This a change in loudness over time in a sound, typically found in synthesizers as ADSR controls: Attack, Decay, Sustain, and Release. In a harmonic sound, the timbre of the sound will usually change over time with the envelope. Sounds with sharp attacks are usually brighter (at least at the beginning).

There is a more important use of the envelope for the mastering engineer, and that is learning tasteful applications of appropriate fades in and out of tracks, also called *tops* and *tails*. This also passes through to the sequencing stage of mastering, in which the whole album is assembled in a (usually) musical manner.

An Introduction to Electricity and Electronics

In electronics, the bundle of functionality is expressed by components bundled into circuits, which are then bundled into functional products.

At the heart of the mastering process is functionality that was formerly the exclusive domain of the physical, or the external mastering chain. To properly understand the virtual desktop mastering chain, we need to have a handle on the functionality of those external devices and how they worked, and how they worked together.

The fundamental building blocks of these signal processors are electronic components, each of which provides physical manipulation ability of somewhat abstract concepts. Each electronic circuit is a physical representation of a mathematical formula: resistors, capacitors, and inductors each have functions or effects whose values are chosen for a given circuit depending on the task that circuit is intended to perform.

There is an evolving process to observe: formerly abstract constructs are physicalized (mathematical formulas to electronic circuits), and formerly physical tasks are virtualized. Printed circuit board design from tape up on Mylar film to CAD (Computer Aided Design), printing and publishing from lead type and large presses to desktop publishing, music generation from symphonies to computers in bedrooms.

There is a movement of task accomplishment—from crude physical formation to fine digital representation—and this is an accelerating function.

Electricity

Electricity begins with atoms, which are composed of a nucleus (containing protons and neutrons), and electrons built up in shells around the nucleus. In electrically stable atoms, the number of protons in the nucleus and the number of electrons in the shells are matched. Good conductors have one extra or one too few electrons in their outermost shell (valence). It is this property that allows electrons to freely move from atom to atom in a conductor.

Electricity is the movement of electrons from atom to atom. The electrons don't move far—just to the next atom—then that atom has too many electrons, and is happy to donate an electron to the next atom. This electron movement is similar to the motion of air molecules by sound pressure. Speakers move air molecules to create sound—so what has to happen to create electron flow?

In 1830, Michael Faraday found out that electron flow (electric current) is generated in a conductor (a wire, typically) by moving it through a magnetic field, so as to cut through magnetic lines of force. The electron flow is "induced" in this way to move through the wire, to create voltage.

Dynamic microphones use induction to generate an audio signal (as do moving coil phono cartridges). Again, when a conductive metal moves in a magnetic field it creates voltage, measured in *volts*. The volt is a unit of measurement used in determining the electrical pressure in a circuit. Voltage is often referred to as *potential*, a difference between two states. Potential energy is the capacity for performing work by virtue of an object or a body's position: for example, a rock held aloft has the potential of falling, whereas a rock on the ground lacks that potential.

In circuits, electrons are forced to move along a desired path, between electrical components and the conductors connecting them. This movement is called *electric current*, which, like water, can move in either direction in an open pipe. When the direction is one way only, we call that direct current (DC). When the current flows back and forth, we call that alternating current (AC). Audio is AC in its essence. The specific speed of the back-and-forth flow (the frequency) passes from component to component, between electrical, mechanical, and atmospheric domains.

Current is the quantity of electricity flowing past a given point at a given time. The force pushing the current is *voltage*. Current is the amount of electricity present in the wires, and *resistance* is the force that reduces current, often while doing work such as lighting a bulb, amplifying a sound, turning a motor, or just generating heat.

When an electric current is passed through a conductor (like a piece of wire), a magnetic field is produced around the wire. It is this interaction and interplay of electron flow and magnetism that is one of the foundations of our electronic devices. If you place a wire with an electric current next to another wire, the wire with the current generates a magnetic field that the next wire will be within, and if that magnetic field moves, a current is induced in the other wire.

Magnetic fields around conductors have a rotation to them, the direction of which depends on which direction current is flowing in the conductor. These magnetic fields rotate in one direction as the current flow increases to its maximum in one direction (end of story for DC), then collapses as the current begins to reverse direction in the wire, and builds up again in the opposite direction in alternating current. This is how transformers work: the building up of the magnetic field in a coil of wire crosses and encompasses a separate wire, which is also wound as a coil with the first wire, inducing a current into the second wire.

The *ampere* (amp) is the unit used to measure the rate of flow of electrical current. Amperage is similar to "gallons per minute" measuring the amount of water passing through a hose. Voltage is similar to how high the water is turned on. The fact that pressure is in the hose does not mean that water is flowing. Voltage (electrical pressure) is not capable of doing any work until there is amperage (current flow).

Disparity between water temperatures can be seen as an example of potential difference as well. Hot and warm water have less potential difference than do hot and ice water. Both of these extremes are measured against room temperature (which in electronics is

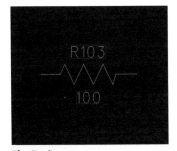

The Resistor

The Potentiometer

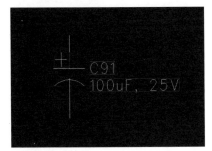

The Capacitor

The Inductor

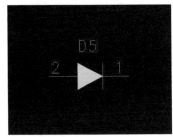

The Diode

referred to as *ground*). This is similar to the role of amplitude in audio: the variations in pressure from the steady-state barometric air pressure in a room are the small variations we call *sound pressure*.

Electronic Components

The electronic "bundle of functionality" is made up of several common components with specific properties and relationships to electron flow. The *resistor* is a two-terminal device that allows either AC or DC to flow through it but blocks the flow by a specific amount, limiting current. Resistance is similar to shrinking the diameter of a garden hose to make the pressure higher (and the flow slower).

There are also three terminal versions of resistors: *variable resistors* (also known as potentiometers, or pots) that are used to vary current or voltage. You see these used for volume and tone controls. A unique version of a resistor is a force sensing resistor (FSR), which varies in resistance based on pressure. An early application of FSRs was for robot fingertips; recently, they are showing up in musical controllers and modular synthesizers. Resistance is measured in *ohms*.

The *capacitor* is a two-terminal device that passes AC and blocks (or impedes) DC, behaving as a reservoir. It stores charge in a dielectric (the bucket) until its capacity is used up, then it waits for the polarity to change, and the electricity flows out in the other direction, emptying the reservoir, filling the capacitor again in the other direction.

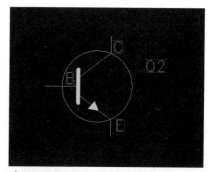

The Transistor

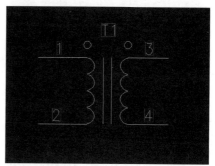

The Transformer

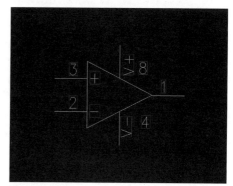

The Op-amp

Normally, capacitors are chosen for a circuit with a high enough capacity to never fill up, since fully filling up for a capacitor is like clipping in audio. The higher the frequency of these polarity changes, the less impedance is presented to the circuit. Polarized capacitors behave like little batteries, always filling up and emptying in the same direction. Capacitance is measured in *farads*.

The *inductor* is a two-terminal device that passes DC but impedes AC. Inductors usually use coils of wire to control the flow of AC: as the current flow changes polarity, the magnetic field around the wire collapses (as the voltage passes zero) and rebuilds again as the current goes the other way. If the current is always going in the same direction (as in DC), the magnetic field builds around the wire and stays in place; it doesn't move, and therefore no impedance is presented to the flow. Inductors are primarily magnetic manipulators, and are measured in *henrys*.

The *diode* is a two-terminal device that allows current to flow in only one direction, and blocks current in the other direction. Diodes in a bridge configuration change alternating current into direct current. This configuration is a common item in power supplies. Light-emitting diodes are another functional type of diode.

The *transistor* is a three-terminal device that can conduct a lot of current from the *collector* pin to the *emitter* pin based on the state of its *base* pin. The transistor can be thought of as a valve in a pipe. The valve determines the amount of flow that passes through the pipe, not how much was in the pipe to begin with. The transistor is a fundamental component of amplifiers.

The *transformer* is two or more coil windings in the same magnetic field that convert AC voltage in one wire into a magnetic field, and in so doing, induces a voltage in the other wire. This only works with AC. A transformer changes voltages by having a different number of turns in the coil winding on one wire or the other. Transformers typically isolate inputs and outputs and are used to block DC current.

The *operational amplifier* (op-amp) is a component that is used in almost all analog audio circuits. They are typically packaged in integrated circuits containing one, two, or four op-amps. In addition to the power pins on the integrated circuit, each op-amp has three connections: one output and two inputs, one of which reverses the polarity of the input voltage. In typical circuit configurations, some of the op-amp's output voltage is fed back into its negative input, which works to dampen and control the output of the amplifier. The op-amp is the fundamental component in microphone preamplifiers and balanced inputs.

Different values of these basic components arranged in many circuit configurations form the majority of the electronic devices we use every day.

Filters

The filter is one of the most fundamental circuits in audio. There are several types that are used separately and in conjunction with each other to perform certain tasks. Here are four common types of filters that are made up of capacitors and inductors:

- *The Highpass Filter:* This type of filter is like a sieve. It lets small, short things (high frequencies) through, but blocks the larger, longer, low frequencies.
- *The Lowpass Filter:* This type of filter allows low frequencies to pass, but blocks high frequencies.
- *The Bandpass Filter:* This type of filter is a combination of a lowpass and a highpass filter. It is configured to allow a portion of the frequency range through, but typically not the low and high frequencies to either side of the center frequency of the filter.
- *The Band Reject Filter:* This is similar to the bandpass, except that the low and high frequencies around its band are allowed through. This is also known as a *notch filter*.

Filters have three characteristics: the *passband*, the *stopband*, and the *transition band*. The passband, in an ideal filter, is that part of the frequency range that is allowed to pass unimpeded. The stopband (again, in an ideal filter) is the part of the frequency range where none shall pass. The transition band is the interface between the two, and ideally would be straight up and down—an instantaneous transition from stopped to passed frequencies.

The transition band's center frequency is typically called the *cutoff frequency*. It has a bandwidth of its own, depending on the steepness of the slope, which is measured in some filters (lowpass and highpass) in decibels per octave, and in other types of filters (bandpass, notch) is termed *Q* or *quality factor*. A high Q is a steep slope, a low Q is not so much. Passbands ideally have fully flat frequency response. The steepness of the cutoff slope of a filter determines the quality and integrity of the signal. The steeper the cutoff slope of a filter, the more ripple in the signal.

Crossovers

A crossover uses two or more filters to divide a full-bandwidth signal into two or more frequency ranges, so that specific frequencies can be matched to specific speakers or be sent to individual signal processors for further manipulation. Any speaker system that has a discrete woofer and tweeter uses a crossover. Large-scale P.A. systems use crossovers to send line-level signals to discrete amps to power the different-frequency-range speaker stacks.

Signal Processor Families

Just as there are several types of components with different characteristics, and different types of filters made from these, there is a family of devices based on the "bundles of functionality" provided by the combinations of the above—the *signal processors*. They take a signal, change it in a highly specific way, and return the signal for further processing if needed. These make up the core of any mastering chain.

Signal processors generally can be grouped into four functions:

1. Amplitude Processors
2. Frequency Processors
3. Frequency and Amplitude Processors
4. Time-Based Processors

Amplitude Processors

This side of the signal-processing family, as the name suggests, deals largely with level and volume—turning it up and down depending on conditions presented by the settings. These are also called *dynamics processors*, and are a type of amplifier.

The *compressor* is one of the most important amplitude processors. Depending on the settings, compressors turn down the incoming signal by a certain amount (set by the ratio control) after the signal reaches a certain level (set by the threshold control). The compressor's action is called *compression*, and it serves to reduce the dynamic range of the signal passing through it.

Now that the signal is turned down at the loudest points, you can turn the whole thing up without clipping; so compressors allow soft sounds to be loud while keeping loud sounds loud as well. This is called taking *output gain*, or *make-up gain*, and is applied after all compression is complete, letting you turn the signal level up without fear of the formerly uncompressed peaks clipping.

One way of looking at a compressor is as though it were a big steamroller hanging from springs above the ground. The audio is going by on a conveyer belt below the roller. If the piled-up audio never reaches the height of the roller, there is no effect on the audio. The roller height above the audio is set by the threshold control. As you bring the threshold of the roller down onto the audio, the heaps start to be flattened off on top. The spring tension is the ratio control. If the ratio is very heavy and stiff (say 10:1), the levels of the audio will be pretty well smooshed down and flattened out. Alternatively, with a quite light spring tension setting (say 2:1), then the roller rides up and down on the level of the audio, just smoothing out the tops of the heaps somewhat.

Compression Punchbag

Another great example of compression can be seen when punching a pillow. If you punch in the direction of a pillow and don't even hit it, there is no effect on your fist. If you strike the pillow, your throw will be absorbed by the pillow, depending on its firmness. Pillow firmness is the ratio in this example; the higher the ratio, the harder the pillow. At some point the pillow loses all softness and becomes a plank of wood. This is the domain of the limiter, described below.

There are other compressor controls that are time based: the attack setting of a compressor sets how long after the threshold is crossed before applying compression. This is handy for letting initial transient (quick) sounds through, then taming the bulk of the louder sound a bit later. A related control is the release setting, which keeps the audio turned down for the length of the setting, even after the threshold has reset.

The *limiter* is a specialized form of compressor that has the ratio set at infinity to 1. In other words, when the level crosses the threshold setting, the output will not increase substantially, no matter how high the input signal spikes. This is like punching the plank—this far, and no farther. This setting is also known as a *brickwall* limiter.

The *expander* is the complement of the compressor. Where a compressor makes loud sounds softer and soft sounds louder, the expander makes loud sounds louder and soft sounds softer. This is one of the key functions in the desktop mastering bundle of functionality.

The *noise gate* can be thought of as a downward expander. If the signal level falls below the threshold level, the volume is turned down. A noise gate has two parameters: threshold and reduction level. Noise gates (more than 1,000 of them) are put to good use in the Noise Reduction section of the mastering chain.

Frequency Processors

This branch of the signal-processing family typically contains special effects, synthesis, or distortion generators.

The *exciter* (or enhancer) adds *harmonic distortion* to a signal to make the signal pop. Harmonic distortion comes in a couple of flavors: even harmonic and odd harmonic. Even harmonics tend to make sounds soft, warm, and full (often associated with tube distortion), while odd harmonics tend to make the sound metallic, hollow, and bright (often associated with solid-state distortion).

The *bass synthesizer* generates or regenerates a tone or a series of harmonics related to the low-frequency input content of the processor, usually an octave above or below the incoming program material. This device typically splits the input with a crossover frequency control (to determine the split point). The frequencies above the split point are sent directly to the output, while the low-end frequencies are analyzed by the processor to generate the additional bass reinforcing tones or harmonics.

Frequency and Amplitude Processors

This branch of the signal-processing family includes some of my favorites: equalizers, multiband compressors, and de-essers.

Equalizers (EQs) let us selectively change the balance of frequencies in a signal. There are several types of equalizers, all based around a few common parameters: *amplitude, frequency, bandwidth* and *Q* or *quality factor.*

Amplitude is the level of boost or cut or gain, measured in decibels, as in +10 dB or –10 dB. This is how much amplification is happening in a given frequency band of an equalizer.

Frequency determines the center frequency of interest, bounded by the bandwidth. For highpass and lowpass shelving EQs, the frequency at which a filter begins to boost or cut.

Bandwidth determines how many specific frequencies around the selected frequency are boosted or cut. Bandwidth is usually measured per octave, from one-twelfth to three octaves.

Q or *quality factor* comes in a couple of different flavors: *constant-Q* or *proportional-Q*. Q is a way to describe how fast a transition from a stopband to a passband is, and is measured as the bandwidth 3 dB below the level of the peak amplitude of the filter. Constant-Q filters maintain a constant bandwidth regardless of the level of the filter. Proportional-Q varies the bandwidth affected by the filter (usually affecting a broad bandwidth at low levels, and peaking into a narrow bandwidth at higher levels). Generally we use Q as a description of the slope of the "skirt" of the EQ.

EQ Types

The *parametric EQ* provides user control of the three main parameters: amplitude, center frequency, and bandwidth. This EQ may also provide high- or low-shelving filters, and by definition can be peaking or notch filter EQs as well. These are called "state variable" equalizers, since the user can vary the state of the parameters.

The *graphic EQ* removes the variability one of these parameters, the center frequency, which provides boost/cut controls for specific frequencies, from 5 to 31 bands. Graphic equalizers are good for quick adjustments and also for permanent adjustments like room tuning; in other words, there is not a lot of fine control because of the lack of frequency-adjustment capability.

The *peaking* or *notch filter* EQ controls the loudness of a single frequency range. These are handy to solve feedback problems, or to remove specific problematic frequencies such as 50- or 60-cycle hum. They are usually set by boosting a given frequency and sweeping the filter along the frequency range until the problem area appears and intensifies, then cutting at that point until the problem frequency is resolved.

The *shelving EQ* controls the loudness of high or low frequencies above or below a fixed frequency. The frequency at which a filter begins to boost or cut is called the cutoff point, and the slope of the filter tapers to flat above (highpass) or below (lowpass) that point.

Multiband compressors are a special breed of processor. They have the multiple frequency bands of an equalizer and the compression ability of compressors. They are also one of the easiest processors to misuse, because of the level of control provided.

When a full-range signal enters a multiband compressor, it is split out using a crossover circuit into however many bands the unit offers (usually between three and five bands). In the desktop mastering chain described in this book, we use the Waves C4 Multiband Parametric Processor, which provides four bands of control.

Typically, there are controls to set the crossover split frequencies that determine the width and frequency coverage of each band, and the standard compression controls of threshold and ratio. A separate solo and bypass are provided so the effect of the processing can be heard in each band on its own.

The *de-esser* is like a shelving or notch filter EQ and a compressor put together. Its stated purpose is to remove sibilance (the hissy *ess* or *sh* sound), usually out of vocals. Sometimes there is simply an excess of high end, and a de-esser is just the ticket to provide high-frequency control. Similar to the bass synthesizer above, the de-esser includes a crossover, which splits the frequency range in two (high and low bands), but passes the low band through unaffected.

Time-Based Processors

Time-based processors mess with linear time, and include reverb and delay (and other processors based on them).

Reverb is a time-based processor that simulates the environment of a reverberant space. It is made up of a series of echoes, closely spaced, with the tone and timbre of the reflections affected, usually by EQ. Reverb is typically made up of several components: the direct signal, early reflections (first reflections from large structures in the simulated environment), and reverberation (many reflections from all surfaces, spaced closely enough in time so that they are not audible as different sounds).

Delay is the repetition of a sound. *Delay* and *echo* are essentially the same thing: a delay repeats once, and an echo repeats several times. In the strictly analog days, delays and echoes were made by a physical distance between a reel-to-reel tape recorder's record and playback heads in effects like the Echoplex tape delay, using magnetic tape to store the audio signal until playback. Then, a discrete-time analog delay line was developed using a series of capacitors in a bucket-brigade arrangement. These capacitance elements filled up with a voltage representing a waveform at a certain point in time, then passing the voltage to the next capacitor in line, refilling from the waveform voltage level presented at the next defined point in time. This created an echo effect, variable in time depending on which capacitor you tapped to reconstruct the voltages back into an audio signal. The bucket-brigade delay was an early form of digital sampling and playback.

These days, delays are created using digital signal processing, and are at the heart of many effects: reverb, chorus, flanging, phasers, loopers, and more have digital delays at their core.

Major Components

All these building blocks are meaningless until there is a playback system to hear them with, which brings us to the two major components of any serious musical endeavor: the amplifier and then on to the speakers.

The Amplifier

The *amplifier* is the piece of gear used most often in a studio. Microphone preamplifiers, equalizers, mixer auxiliary sends, dynamics processors, pan pots, and faders are all controlling or are functionally based on amplifiers. Any time you hear something over headphones or through speakers, an amplifier provides the motive power for the speakers.

In an amplifier, a small amount of energy (the audio signal) regulates a large amount of energy (the current from the power supply in the unit—and ultimately the AC plug). If this sounds like the description of the transistor, it should. Amplifiers are based on the same principle. Let's take a look at the properties and types of amplifiers.

Properties of Amplifiers

Linearity in an amplifier refers to the resemblance of an output to an input; an amp with a perfect linear response responds to all frequencies equally, rather than favoring one over another (which is the job of the equalizer). A perfect linear response is referred to as a *flat response*—what goes in is what comes out. But real amplifiers are not perfect and are linear only within limits. For instance, if you overload the input of an amplifier, the output will go into clipping, which results in a very different output than what was input.

Unity gain refers to an amplifier with zero gain, outputting a signal identical to its input. This property is useful in signal processors and mixing consoles, where signals can be combined without changing their original gain.

Saturation happens when an amplifier does not have enough power to reproduce the signal it receives at its input, and the amplifier becomes saturated and clipping results. We hear clipping as distortion, mostly with odd (unmusical) harmonics.

Power as seen in an amplifier's power rating (which is expressed in watts) can be ideally obtained by multiplying its current and voltage usage. However, since no circuit is 100 percent efficient (and most are a lot less efficient than that), amps typically won't operate at their ideal rated potential. The most accurate way to measure an amplifier's power output is to use root-mean-square (RMS) values.

Slew rate is the speed at which an amplifier can change the amplitude of its output signal, and it is measured in V/ms (volts/microsecond), with a higher figure being a faster response. A faster response indicates a more accurate representation of the input signal. Low-power amplifiers (up to 100W per channel) should have a slew rate if at least 10 V/ms. High-power amplifiers (over 200W) should have a slew rate of at least 30 V/ms.

Signal-to-Noise Ratio expresses the range between the amplifier's nominal output and the quietest signal it can accurately reproduce. This ratio is expressed in decibels.

Dynamic Range expresses the range between the amplifier's maximum undistorted output and the quietest signal it can accurately reproduce, and is expressed in decibels.

Types of Amplifiers

In addition to op-amps, crossovers, equalizers, and dynamics processors described above, there are several other types of amplifiers to be aware of.

The *preamplifier* takes a low-level signal and amplifies it so that it is usable by other electronics, typically to *line level*. Low-level signal sources include microphones, guitar pickups, and turntables. Other preamplifier types take multiple line-level inputs and switch between them.

A *phono preamp* also adds an equalization playback curve (called the RIAA curve) to compensate for the equivalent but opposite curve used when a record is cut. This curve, during vinyl record creation, keeps the low-frequency motion of the groove minimized (too much of which would throw the needle out of the groove) and amplifies high frequencies, increasing their resolution for accurate reproduction. On the playback side, low-frequencies are amplified back up (potentially increasing low-frequency issues like rumble), and high frequencies are turned down (along with record noise and hiss).

Summing amplifiers receive signals from a number of sources and combine them at unity gain while completely isolating each source, preventing any leakage from other signals upstream. These are used in mixers or in any device where two or more analog signals are combined. They are also used to take outputs from multichannel audio interfaces to get more headroom and performance, using all of the output stages rather than having all the channels summed inside the interface to the stereo outputs.

Distribution amplifiers take a single signal and split it into multiple signals, usually at unity gain. This is called a *buffered multiple* in modular synthesis, as compared with a *multiple*, which is just a bunch of jacks wired together in parallel.

Differential amplifiers are used for balanced inputs and outputs. These are typically made from op-amps, which on the input side have two inputs: one positive and one negative. A positive polarity waveform comes into the positive terminal, and a negative polarity waveform is on the negative terminal. This amplifier amplifies only what is different between the two inputs—hence the name differential amplifier. The benefit that this bestows is in noise rejection. Any noise picked up on the way into a differential input is rejected, as it is the same on both inputs, and only what is different is amplified.

Power amplifiers amplify line-level audio signals to a signal that will drive speakers. They require more current than do most other audio devices.

12

Conclusion

I am blessed with interesting eyes. I am farsighted in my left eye—I have good focus beyond arm's length. I am nearsighted in my right eye, and have good focus inside of arm's length. This provides good focus throughout the range of vision. At every distance, I have one good focus and one not so good, adding light to the situation, but not clarity.

I received my first pair of glasses at 22 years of age. Until the day I put them on, I didn't know I was missing something. I could see everything in focus and was impressed that TV looked so much like real life. When the glasses went on, I received the gift of parallax—and with it, depth perception. The interesting thing is that nothing changed except for my perception.

The outside world did not change (but I spent three months ogling the corners of the room). My eyes did not change—just my tools of perception and my awareness of a new dimension.

The act of listening can be like this as well: there is a depth to music, sound, and audio that exists outside of ourselves, and that we can train to perceive. It is concentrated attention that provides eyeglasses to our ears.

Multidimensional Vision

As artists we learn to see. As children we learn what not to see. The multitude of detail surrounding us is overpowering, especially for babies who have so much to learn all at once.

Media is fast approaching a saturation point, which gives us a great evolutionary kick and an opportunity to practice multidimensional vision. Here is an example that applies to all of us:

On a clear night, look to the stars. What do you see? Are you seeing a large black cloth pierced with holes, with the light of heaven shining through? Some people still view the skies with two-dimensional vision. A necessary step in mastering and in seeing reality is to understand the many levels of detail contained in what we see and hear.

Now look to the stars and see the huge fireballs placed relatively near or extremely far from you. You can picture the view in three dimensions, a giant lattice containing a multitude of points. The brightest stars may not be the closest to us.

The stars that are visible to the naked eye range from around 4 light-years to 5,000 light-years away from the Earth. This means that the light you are seeing was generated between 4 and 5,000 years ago, allowing you a view in a fourth dimension: time. This spread of vision over time poses an interesting point: we really aren't seeing things all at the same time. Since the light from near objects hits our eye before the light from farther objects, even looking down a wall gives us a spread of time. This usually isn't relevant in our everyday life, but it is true.

This gives us two, three, and four dimensions to see a familiar sight with. We can even think about one-dimensional vision with the stars. Each of those fusion fireballs is releasing energy in all directions! What we are seeing is just the line between the star and our eye.

That star would be as bright from the same distance in any direction. If there were a huge reflector behind the stars we see, this would be a very bright place indeed.

Windup

There is an external virtual global consciousness developing, already underway. You are a part of it. Be a good part. Since you have read this book, you are probably part of the hearing center, called the "mastering engineer." See what needs doing, and do it. Post everywhere. Read everything.

There is a hermetic saying that goes "As above, so below, and as below, so above." This presents the "law of similarity" and the concept of universal truths. Where this can help us is that universal truths, by definition, are in everything we do and learn. This allows us to apply templates of systems to other systems. For example, the chain of making a song—from composition to tracking to mixing to mastering to release to consumption—has a similarity to the subset of that process that is the desktop mastering chain. Each stage needs to be properly prepared for the next—that is an example of a universal truth.

The more you do and learn, try to identify the aspects of your work that are transferable to other parts of your life. Truly, mastering your music is like mastering your life.

Be a sense organ of the global consciousness—imagine how many square miles of CCD chips have been manufactured into digital cameras—that is its retina. Your social graph is a neural net, and your data cascade is the synaptic flow.

Every word you write on the Internet becomes a memory of the global consciousness, which has perfect recall. Conduct yourself appropriately, and represent yourself as you wish your grandchildren and great-grandchildren to know you.

Presingularity, the world is akin to a hungover frat boy, passed out on the floor. It is our job to self-organize and wake up. It has already started, and you are already a part of it. The singularity is when this virtual global consciousness wakes up and we become responsible parts of one interconnected entity, doing the work of our hearts' desire.

Everything happens at exactly the right time to get to where we are now. The most important decision you have to make is your next one, including how deep a breath to take.

Audio Taxonomy: A Glossary of Subtle Terms

Communication is among the highest skills required for working well with other people. One of the necessities for efficient communication is a shared vocabulary. Audio, in general, and high-end audio in particular, suffers from a plethora of ill-defined, nebulous terms.

The following is a short list of descriptions that I asked my good friend and mentor Patrick Donicht to assemble for me, and I am quite pleased with the results.

3D. Sounds seem to move outside of the speakers to the left and right and from front to back.

body. The feeling that something substantial is there in the sound.

bright. Too much high-frequency energy or not enough low-frequency energy.

colored. Audio-processing equipment that imparts a distinct tonal character to the recorded sound.

depth. The ability to place instruments front and back in a mix.

distant. Having too much reverb.

distortion. Clipping or overdriving a circuit. Distortion can be good or bad, depending on the desired results or harmonics.

dull (or dark). Having very little high-frequency energy.

fatiguing. Makes you want to stop listening after a relatively short time.

harsh. Irritating sounds coming from your monitors that cause cringing, quickly sending pets and/or spouses out of the room. This is also known as an ice pick to the ear, usually found in the 3K range.

imaging. Presenting a left and right sense within a mix, as in a stereo image.

masking. When an abundance of one frequency range overshadows another. Noise like hum, hiss, and so on can create a masking effect.

muddy (or boomy). Too much bass in the 160 to 220 Hz range.

muffled. Welcome to 500 Hz world. This is a frequency range good at masking.

scooped. Missing the midrange frequencies. This is also called the *loudness* or *smile* curve.

smooth (or neutral). Describes a pleasant listening experience with no single frequency range sticking out.

taking gain. To turn something up.

thin. Lacking bass and depth.

tops and tails. To trim and add appropriate fades to the beginning and ending of a mastered track.

transparent. Used when describing audio-processing equipment that imparts little or no change to the original sound.

warm (or thick). A balanced frequency response across the frequency range with emphasis in the bass range and no lack of clarity.

UltraViolet Studios Discography

Date Completed	Artist	Project
12/11/1997	Colour Twigs	*Sticks and Stoned*
1/1/1998	Gordon Raphael	*The Lost City/Lifetimes*
5/24/1998	The Cowboys	*Jet City Rockers*
6/7/1998	The Heats	*Smoke*
9/21/1998	Riverside Church	*Christmas Pageant*
9/29/1998	Violet Transmission	*Violet Transmission*
12/18/1998	Corporal Blossom	*Corporal Blossom*
12/27/1998	Bryan TCD Training	Audio restoration
1/31/1999	Chinas Comidas	Chinas Comidas EP
2/20/1999	Youth for Christ Sheback Choir	*Youth for Christ Sheback Choir*
4/25/1999	Chris Gillette	Chris Gillette EP
9/7/1999	The U-Men	*Solid Action*
9/27/1999	Phreeworld	*Across the Sound*
1/9/2000	Electron Love Theory	Power of the People EP
1/30/2000	Electron Love Theory	*Electron Love Theory*
6/28/2000	Supernot	*Supernot*
10/16/2000	El Grande Conquistador	El Grande Conquistador EP
3/10/2001	Mr. Rudi	*Don't Hold Back*
5/3/2001	Electron Love Theory	*Colors of the Galaxy*
5/18/2001	Ashcan School	*Ashcan School*
5/19/2001	Whisenhaut Family	Cassette cleanup and transcription
5/28/2001	Juana Camilleri	*Palisades*
6/28/2001	Norman Durkee	*NeoCool*
6/28/2001	Norman Durkee	*EG Girls 1, EG Girls 3, EG Girls 3*
7/21/2001	Rye	Toast EP

Date Completed	Artist	Project
8/30/2001	Pigeonhed	Unreleased CD
9/20/2001	David Miles Huber	*Haida*
10/26/2001	Rag N Boom	*Rag N Boom*
11/16/2001	Downtown Composers Collective	Sears commercial
12/21/2001	Downtown Composers Collective	BMW commercial
12/21/2001	Downtown Composers Collective	Newsday commercial
12/27/2001	The Holidays	*Big Sexy World*
1/4/2002	STS	Audio restoration
1/26/2002	Downtown Composers Collective	AT&T demo
2/8/2002	Wayne Horowitz	*Zony Mash: Live in Seattle*
2/17/2002	CUT-OUT	*Interlude with Fun Machine*
4/27/2002	King Crimson	*Live 3/10/1972 The Barn—Peoria, IL*
4/27/2002	King Crimson	*Live 2/19/1972 Grande Ballroom—Chicago, IL*
4/27/2002	King Crimson	*Live 2/18/1972 Grande Ballroom—Detroit, MI*
4/27/2002	King Crimson	*Live 2/17/1972 Grande Ballroom—Detroit, MI*
4/27/2002	King Crimson	*Live 2/11/1972 Armoury— Wilmington, DE*
4/27/2002	King Crimson	*Live 2/12/1972 Academy of Music—New York, NY*
4/27/2002	King Crimson	*Live 2/27/1972 Kemp Coliseum—Orlando, FL*
4/27/2002	King Crimson	*Live 10/13/1972 Zoom Club—Frankfurt, Germany*
6/29/2002	Jeth Odom	*The Absence of Theory*

Date Completed	Artist	Project
7/5/2002	Jacob Taylor	*Jacob Taylor*
7/18/2002	I DEFY	*I DEFY*
8/1/2002	The Fading Collection	*Interactive Family Radio*
8/20/2002	Scott Adams	*Birds May Bite*
11/4/2002	El Grande Conquistador	*Private Radio Sessions*
11/12/2002	Steve Pearson	*Battles and Ballads*
11/25/2002	Atomic Chamber Ensemble	*ACE*
12/18/2002	Norman Durkee	Helen Keller double 7" EP
1/7/2003	Walter Harley	*Thornton Creek*
1/23/2003	Pinehurst Kids	Pinehurst Kids EP
2/26/2003	Steve Fisk	Producer reel (demo)
5/22/2003	The Authorities	Foreveready 7" EP
5/23/2003	Mische Eddins	*Vertebrae No. 5*
5/28/2003	Carissa's Wierd	*Ugly But Honest*
5/28/2003	Carissa's Wierd	*You Should Be at Home Here*
6/6/2003	Probono	*Spilt Milk*
6/26/2003	One Carper Green	One Carper Green EP
7/6/2003	Downtown Composers Collective	K2 commercial
7/21/2003	Steve Ball	*Steve Ball Roadshow*
8/25/2003	Sameer Shukla	Sameer Shukla EP
9/15/2003	T.O.P.	
10/16/2003	Valor's Minon	*Prelude to Legacy*
10/21/2003	Jake Perrine	*VAMP Rock Opera* soundtrack
11/10/2003	The Fading Collection	*Stems*
12/29/2003	Ron Sonntag	*Snohomish Storm*
1/2/2004	Analog Dreamer	*Allure Fiction*
2/6/2004	Downtown Composers Collective	NASA trailer
3/8/2004	Oh'Rion	*Oh'Rion*

Date Completed	Artist	Project
3/10/2004	Numeriklab	*Numeriklab*
3/24/2004	Mirkwood	*Dead Young Poets*
5/14/2004	Trevor Reichman	Tre EP
6/9/2004	Garrett Driscoll	*Garrett Driscoll*
6/10/2004	Red Letter Ransom	*Red Letter Ransom*
7/14/2004	Neon	*Neon*
7/22/2004	Cold Water Romance	*Cold Water Romance*
8/9/2004	Steve Fisk	*Shards*
8/16/2004	Numeriklab	*Signals*
9/12/2004	Beehive	*Cycle A*
10/7/2004	Magnus Svennson	*Schumann and Kokkonen*
10/22/2004	Opher Yisraeli	License tracks
11/3/2004	John Woodworth	*Unleaded*
11/7/2004	Jeremy Winters	*Baby Robot Nursery*
11/8/2004	ESITU	*ESITU*
11/19/2004	Carl Tippens	*Carl Tippens*
11/26/2004	Under the Lake	*UTL*
12/14/2004	The Amish Cowboys	Cassette capture and remaster
12/19/2004	Margaret F	*Nocturne*
12/21/2004	The Decibel Collective	Master entire licensing library (6,000 tracks)
1/11/2005	Maximillion Keene	*A Couple Weeks After*
1/18/2005	Al Larson	*The Hardline According to Danny & the Dinosaur*
2/1/2005	Today of Days	Today of Days EP
4/3/2005	The Toms	*Toms Greatest Hits* (Bonus Disc)
4/30/2005	Adventuress	*Adventuress*
5/10/2005	Seamine	*Seamine*
5/11/2005	Deesis	*Deesis*
5/25/2005	Mercir	Instrumentals
6/29/2005	Marsh Gooch	*Lectric Chairs*

Date Completed	Artist	Project
7/11/2005	Downtown Composers Collective	Master entire licensing library (500 tracks)
8/27/2005	Spaceship X	*I Love the Aliens*
9/2/2005	Sextus	*Singles*
9/4/2005	Hipbone	*Tried to Make It Work*
9/6/2005	Magnus Svennson	*Resounding Joy*
10/4/2005	Moog Cookbook	*Bartell*
10/12/2005	Jess Gaedke	*Spain*
11/6/2005	Seeing Blind	*Urgency*
11/17/2005	Taste This Northwest	*Taste This Northwest* compilation CD
12/11/2005	Thomas Laramee	*Woke Up Today*
1/3/2006	Susan Palmer	*The Guitar Lesson Companion* (book with CD)
1/7/2006	Such Sweet Thunder	Cassette capture and remaster
2/1/2006	Mercir	*Wind Chimes & Land Mines*
3/28/2006	Miracle Workers	*Live with Long Hair*
4/24/2006	One Reel	2006 Seattle Fireworks soundtrack
4/26/2006	Shane Sasnow	*Shane Sasnow*
5/4/2006	PoP is ArT	*Epiphany*
5/8/2006	Redmond Teen Center	*Sound the Alarm: The Old Redmond Firehouse, Media Lab Compilation #1*
5/13/2006	Katie Davis	*Faraway*
5/22/2006	Monster Buck	*Land of Makebelievers*
5/24/2006	BOBCATS	*Dance.GO.*
5/30/2006	The Lowdown Ramblers	*The Lowdown Ramblers*
6/3/2006	Not Lame	*Buffalo Springfield Tribute: Five Way Street*

Date Completed	Artist	Project
6/6/2006	Meagin Donovan	Meet My Monster EP
6/7/2006	Peter Bagge	*The Action Suits*
7/16/2006	Seamine	*Does Anyone Else Miss the Cold War?*
7/25/2006	Fourth World	*Sensing Danger*
8/22/2006	The Nervous Freemasons	*Live at Chop Suey*
10/9/2006	The Fog People	*City of Night*
10/22/2006	Portage Bay Big Band	*Swingin' in the Rain*
11/4/2006	Lost Pedro	*Lost Pedro*
11/8/2006	Glass Republic	*Glass Republic*
11/12/2006	The Nervous Freemasons	*Nervus Ordo Seclorum*
11/15/2006	The Nervous Freemasons	*Order Out Of Chaos: Live from Mr. Spot's Chai House*
1/17/2007	Burning Sky Records	Hello! Jellyfish Tribute EP
3/23/2007	Studfinder	*Echinacea Darlin'*
3/29/2007	One Reel	2007 Seattle Fireworks soundtrack
4/1/2007	Ameritrash	*Broken*
4/2/2007	Optimus Rhyme	*He Dies in Rocket School*
4/8/2007	Thomas Laramee	*Seven Shades of Time*
4/17/2007	Danielli	*Haters Heart*
5/2/2007	Shoreline CC Sonic Arts	*Sonic Arts 2007*
5/15/2007	Johnny Illness	"79"
5/18/2007	Studfinder	*Ouchie Meow Meow*
6/13/2007	Steve Pearson	*British Racing Green*
7/10/2007	The Protocol	*Recess*
7/23/2007	Burning Sky Records	*Sensory Lullabies: Jellyfish Tribute* (2 CDs)
8/13/2007	Burning Sky Records	*Sensory Lullabies: Bonus CD*
8/15/2007	Brian Marshall	*Unfinished Thoughts*
9/12/2007	Sextus	*Stranger Than Fiction*

Date Completed	Artist	Project
10/24/2007	Corrugated Films	Movie soundtrack processing
11/28/2007	Maxi Dunn	*Winter Ghost*
12/18/2007	B-Girl	*Love or Fate*
12/28/2007	Barsuk Records	*Kurt Cobain: About a Son* soundtrack
2/13/2008	Burning Sky Records	Beautiful Escape Is Coming Right Along EP
3/17/2008	Burning Sky Records	*Beautiful Escape: Posies Tribute* (3 CDs)
3/19/2008	One Reel	2008 Seattle Fireworks soundtrack
4/3/2008	Maxi Dunn	Gravitational Seed EP
4/3/2008	Amelia Ray	*ON*
4/25/2008	Charlotte Pop Festival	2008 Charlotte Pop Fest compilation CD
6/10/2008	The Smith Bros.	*Indecision*
7/16/2008	UBIK.	*The World Is a Glorious Biomechanical Nightmare*
8/28/2008	Amandala	*Tanzanite*
9/29/2008	Andra Riffle	*Awakening*
9/30/2008	Electron Love Theory	*In the Shadows of U2*
11/15/2008	4th World	*Hidden Path*
1/10/2009	Optimus Rhyme	*Transformed*
1/12/2009	The Fallen	*The Fallen*
3/12/2009	One Reel	2009 Seattle Fireworks soundtrack
3/20/2009	Calleye Productions	*Beyond Greenaway* movie soundtrack
3/24/2009	Michel Drucker Expérience	*Le Grand Voyage*
4/27/2009	Ill Divine	*Ill Divine*
5/5/2009	Shai Azul	*Mirror Darkly*
6/6/2009	The Calculus Affair	*The Calculus Affair*

Date Completed	Artist	Project
7/15/2009	Burning of I	*Nowhere Is a Destination*
7/27/2009	Luc and the Lovingtons	*Feel the Warmth*
8/2/2009	Burning Sky Records	*Take Refuge in Pleasure: Roxy Music Tribute* (3 CDs)
8/12/2009	Olympic Sound Collective	*OSC Live in Seattle*
8/19/2009	Maxi Dunn	*Welcome to Soonville*
8/25/2009	Tom Laramee	*Again*
9/3/2009	Charlotte Pop Festival	2009 Charlotte Pop Fest compilation CD
9/29/2009	Thunder Buffalo	*Thunder Buffalo*
10/2/2009	Turn 10 Studios	*Forza Motorsport 3* original soundtrack CD
10/4/2009	Cliff Riffle	*Patience of a Seed*
10/22/2009	Edgar Jiménez P.	*Edgar Jiménez con el Sentimiento Muerto*
10/27/2009	Frank Royster	*Innocence Is Bliss*
11/10/2009	The Sexy Accident	"Jest"
11/10/2009	Los Pixel	*Cuanto Cuesta*
11/23/2009	Tommi Zender	*Words Get in the Way*
1/23/2010	David Stace-James	*Piano Soundtrack*
2/13/2010	Laurie Biagini	*A Far-Out Place*
2/20/2010	Wehrwolve	*Interstellar Spaceports Lost*
3/15/2010	Disciples of Pop	*Disciples of Pop*
3/16/2010	Stitch in Time	*Live at Club Motor*
4/19/2010	One Reel	2010 Seattle Fireworks soundtrack
5/18/2010	Paul Lesinski	*A Fear of Flashing Light*
5/19/2010	Paul Ellis	*Watch the Stars Come One by One*
5/26/2010	Make Phantoms	*Make Phantoms*
6/2/2010	James Deane and the Rebels	*PROD*

Date Completed	Artist	Project
8/1/2010	Scott Moore	*The Accidental Markers*
8/2/2010	Meagin Donovan	*No Second Self*
8/27/2010	The Volcano Diary	*The Volcano Diary*
9/8/2010	Carbon111	*Stealing the Sun*
9/26/2010	Curt Golden	*(scream)*
9/29/2010	Elbow Coulee	*Elbow Coulee*
10/2/2010	Monster Buck	*Jockey Down*
10/7/2010	More Than Lester	*The Great Equalizer*
11/5/2010	Can You Imagine?	*Can You Imagine?*
11/5/2010	Tin Shed	*Tin Shed*
11/12/2010	Thomas Hunter	*White China Gold*
12/18/2010	The Magic IF	Cassette capture and remaster
1/25/2011	Paul Manousos	*The Strongbox Diaries*
2/3/2011	Red Martian	*Slow Motion Samurai*
2/3/2011	Marc Silber	*Demystified Bliss*
2/6/2011	Such Sweet Thunder	4-cassette capture and remaster for 4-disc box set
3/1/2011	Imperial Drag	*Out of the Closet*—4-disc box set—demos and live
3/2/2011	Lyre	*Iconoclast*
3/4/2011	Ticktockman	*Ticktockman*
3/9/2011	Burning Sky Records	*Stitched Up!! The Songs of Toy Love Revisited*
3/12/2011	One Reel	2011 Seattle Fireworks soundtrack
3/25/2011	Maxi Dunn	*The Neglected Gambit*
4/5/2011	Glenn Crytzer and his Syncopators	*Harlem Mad*
4/16/2011	Susan Palmer	*The New Guitar Lesson Companion* (CD with book)

Date Completed	Artist	Project
4/19/2011	Burning Sky Records	*If I... If I... If I... The Songs of Squeeze Revisited* (4 discs)
4/27/2011	Martin Rebolledo	*Fell*
4/30/2011	4nStereo	4nStereo
5/23/2011	Julie C.	*Sliding Scale*

Acknowledgments

First, thank you for reading this book. I hope it comes at a good time for you, and makes your world a better place. Second, thanks to my publisher, Hal Leonard, and my developmental editor, Bill Gibson, for the opportunity to present it to you. My brother Dave Turnidge read and corrected many early drafts of this book, and it is much better because of him—thank you, Dave!

I've been extremely fortunate over the course of my life to receive the gifts of knowledge provided by a wide range of authors and musicians, each of whom have enriched my life beyond measure. In particular I would like to thank Craig Anderton and Ray Miller, who each sparked my interest in audio electronics and technology at a young age. Ray also was so kind to fact-check the more technical aspects of the manuscript.

Probably the person most responsible for whatever depth of knowledge I possess in the audio field is Dennis Bohn, who I worked with and for in the engineering department of Rane Corporation. Another thing Dennis did for me was to hire Bob Moses as an engineer at Rane, and Bob has become one of the best engineering mentors one could have.

I would never have set foot on the path of mastering if it were not for the advice of Craig Rosenberg, who was the first person to actually answer the question: What is mastering? Also, thanks to Michael Stein and Gordon Raphael for presenting the first opportunity to apply the answer I received and develop my own desktop mastering chain.

Over these years of desktop mastering (since 1998), I've had friends that have become good clients, and clients that have become good friends. Among many others, these long-term supporters include Jeff Leisawitz and Steve Fisk.

Christian Heilman is the producer and cocreator with me of The Ars Divina Metaphysical Experience, whose mixes are found on the accompanying DVD-ROM. Christian provided the gateway to actually making music again. Thanks Christian!

Alan Heaton is my partner in Burning Sky Records, which fueled my mastering business to the global reach it has now, as well as provided projects based on and paying tribute to some of my favorite artists.

Last, but the farthest from least, my wife of more than 30 years, Julie Turnidge, has been a steady partner in enabling my heart's desire and the alignment of my vocation and avocation. Thanks are also due for her infinite patience while clients march in and out of our home. She is also my best friend, and my relationship with her is truly my highest reward.

The *Desktop Mastering* Companion DVD-ROM

The included DVD-ROM has six directories—each with a 24-bit/44.1 premastered track for you to practice mastering in your own studio. Each directory contains several files:

1. The 44.1/24 bit premaster ready for mastering.
2. The same file, mastered and quantized to 16 bit, with tops and tails trimmed.
3. A series of PNG image files detailing the desktop mastering plug-in chain used to master the file. (See the following six figures.)

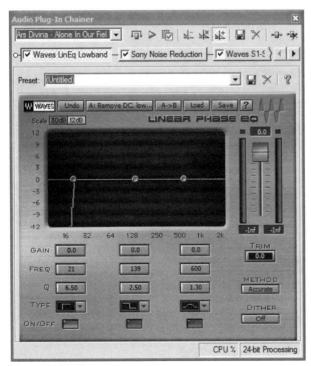

LinEQ Lowband

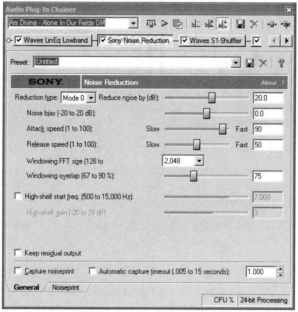

Noise Reduction—General

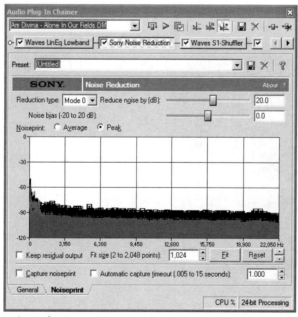

Noise Reduction—Noiseprint

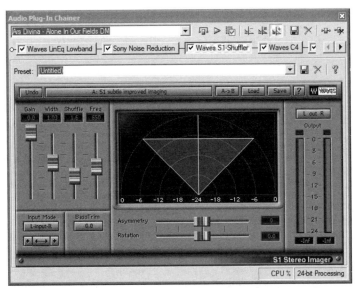

S1 Stereo Imager

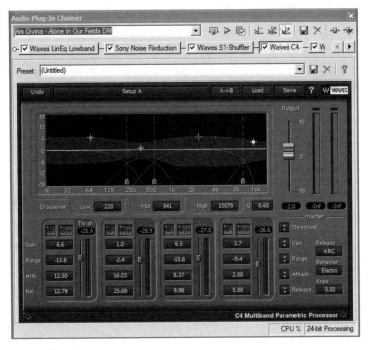

C4 Multiband Parametric Processor

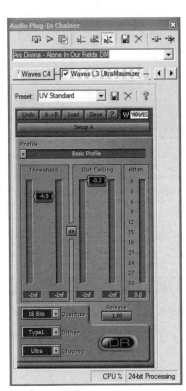

L3 UltraMaximizer

4. Two PNG image files showing the premaster and mastered files zoomed out in Sound Forge showing examples of ideal premaster levels and the resulting master levels.

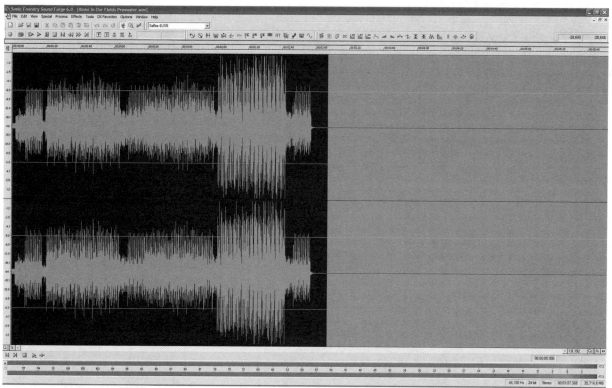

Optimal Premaster Levels

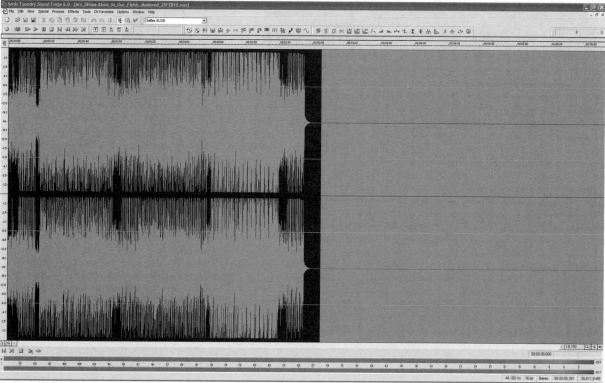

Postmaster Levels

5. An MP4 video for each track showing the critical settings of the C4 plug-in with the ballistics display of the DynamicLine. Also shown in the video is the live moving waveform (on the right) of the premaster prior to the desktop mastering chain and on the left of the screen the Mastered version (see the figure below). In addition, a live real-time analyzer display is shown to visually reinforce the audio frequencies you are hearing. The video shows the most important visual information available when mastering (watching and tuning this plug-in is my primary mastering task). Watching the files go by also provides nonverbal training about what waveforms look like—the density of high frequencies and the large open areas of low frequencies.

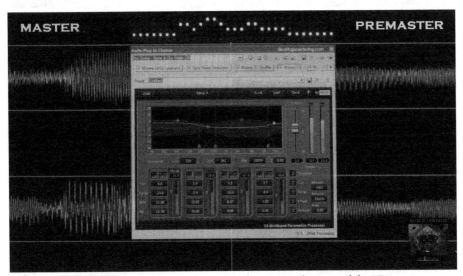

Video Screen Shot of the Premaster Wave, the C4, the Mastered Wave and the RTA.

The Start Noise

Another feature of the videos is to show the action of the *start noise*. You'll notice at the beginning of each video the C4 in the "non-threshold state" (as seen in the Pre-Start Noise figure below) and the start noise energizing each band, preparing the plug-in for the beginning of the track to come (the Post-Start Noise figure). The provided premaster files each have the start noise set at the beginning.

Pre-Start Noise

Post-Start Noise

Watching the Videos

There are a couple of things to keep in mind and to pay attention to while watching the videos. This is the primary task I have as a mastering engineer—looking at the plug-ins while listening to the music and adjusting them accordingly. I don't have the benefit of the moving waveform displays while I am mastering, but there is a lot of information to be derived from watching them. Likewise, the RTA display is front and center while I am mastering. Watching the RTA is like calibrating my ears—is what I am hearing matching up with the frequencies showing on the RTA? These listening and analysis skills are gained over many hours of paying attention to these types of displays.

When you are listening to a premastered track through the plug-in chain, the mastered track is ultimately what you are hearing. That is why we chose to have the mastered tracks as audio for the videos. You may (and should) notice discrepancies between what you are hearing and what you are seeing—for instance, the mastered tracks have been topped and tailed, and the waveform image of the premaster may still be going strong as the mastered file fades out.

The Wave Files

Listening to the premastered and mastered wave files should provide many insights. The premastered files may appear to lack punch and depth—this is a good thing, providing a neutral palette for the desktop mastering chain to work with. Please have a go at mastering these tracks, and I am interested to hear what you come up with!

Index

16-bit   20, 22–24, 27–28, 34, 48, 83–84, 88–89, 91

24-bit   20, 22–24, 27–29, 34, 43, 48, 52, 83–84, 87–89, 91, 185

air pressure   20, 27, 59, 139–140, 156

Alan Heaton   109, 183

alchemist   30

Alesis Masterlink   41, 43

Alexander Graham Bell   146

alias   20

aliasing   21–22

alternating current (AC)   59, 154–155, 157

amperage   155

amplifier   2, 10, 26–27, 59, 125, 152, 157–159, 164–166

amplitude   22, 59, 60, 116–117, 120, 147–150, 156, 159, 161–162, 165

amplitude processors   159, 161

amplitude resolution   22

analog   19, 22–23, 59, 83–84, 157, 163, 166

analog-to-digital converters   19, 59

anti-aliasing filters   21

archival mastering   1

articulation   5, 12, 74, 78, 83

artist name   39, 48, 97, 103

asymmetry   69

attack   5, 52, 54, 67, 76–78, 92–94, 152, 160

Audio Engineering Society   57, 132, 134

audio interface   10, 14, 166

audio waveform   16

automotive systems   7

backup   17–18, 51

balance   3–7, 16, 25–26, 31, 40, 48, 59, 62, 69, 76, 82, 87, 161, 172

ballistics   76, 78–79, 189

band reject filter   158

bandpass filter   158

bandwidth   20, 73, 144, 158–159, 161–162

bass   5, 10, 15–16, 27, 40, 56, 58, 62, 63, 70–71, 76–77, 161, 163, 172

bass guitar   27, 40

bass management   15

bass synthesizer   161, 163

binary   3, 19, 20, 83

bit   6, 20, 23, 84–85, 87

bit depth   6, 22–24

black noise   11, 143

boominess   6, 16, 26, 69, 71, 83

Brad Marvin   126

brand   48, 49, 125, 129

brown noise   11

bucket-brigade delay   164

Buffalo Springfield Tribute   108–109, 177

buggy whips   7

bundle of functionality   3, 7–8, 74, 124, 135, 137, 153, 156, 161

Burning Sky Records   49, 109–110, 135, 137, 178–182, 183

business card binder   128

business cards   107, 125, 128, 132, 134

business insurance   129

business license   129

C4 Parametric Processor   52, 58

C4 PreThreshold Droop   53

C4 time-lapse image   53

capacitors   153, 157–158, 163

car stereo   15

career overview box set   110

CD Architect .wav file   103

CD Baby   110

CD unmuting time   93

CD-TEXT   101, 103

Charlotte Pop Festival   107, 179–180

Chris Porter   118

Chuckie-Boy Records   112, 175

clicks 62, 92–94

client and opportunity base are infinite 121, 124, 133

client contact and recruitment 132

client environment 132

client video monitor 16, 132

clipping 4–5, 34, 44–45, 82–83, 108, 108, 150, 152, 157, 160, 164, 165, 171

clock 19–20

cloud computing 18

Colour Twigs: 31, 65, 173

comments are currency 137

communication 27, 39, 41, 132, 171

compact disc (CD) 2, 6, 15, 21, 24, 26, 40–41, 45–48, 51, 55, 82, 93, 98, 99–101, 103, 106, 107–108, 110–112, 114, 118; 125, 132

compilation CD 106

complex waveforms 149

compression 5–6, 23, 29, 44, 73, 79–81, 116, 142, 159–160, 162–163

compressor, defined 159–160

computer 3, 9–10, 14, 17, 24, 49, 66, 144, 153

computer video cards 24

consonant harmonics 149

constant-Q 162

constructive failure 125

count-ins 92

crossfades 100

crossover 73, 77, 144, 159, 161, 163

cutdowns 118

cutoff slopes 21

dBFS 146

dBpoweramp 98

DC offset 57–60

decay 85, 152

decibel (dB) 5, 34, 71, 74, 78, 146–147, 158, 161, 165

de-esser 5, 74, 79, 83, 161, 163

delay 115, 125, 148, 163–164

Derek Sivers 110

desktop mastering chain 3–4, 23, 57–58, 77–78, 131, 153, 163, 169, 183, 189, 191

destructive interference 70

differential amplifiers 59, 166

digital audio 3, 17, 19, 21–22, 24, 66, 143 146, 149

Digital Music News 128

dimension 23, 38, 68, 138, 140–142, 167–168

diode 155, 157

direct current (DC) 154

dissonant harmonics 149

distribution amplifiers 166

dither 6, 23, 57, 83–85, 89, 103

dither and the 9th bit 84

dog 39, 40

download directory 51

Dropbox.com 48–49

dynamic microphones 154

dynamic range 4, 23, 66, 83, 87, 159, 165

dynamics processors 159, 164–165

early reflections 163

echo 163–164

Echoplex tape delay 163

Elbert Hubbard 123

electric current 154–155

electricity and electronics 153

electronic components 156

electrons 154

energy vampire 125

envelope 62, 93, 152

EQ magazine 131

equalization 2, 4–5, 165

equalizer 12, 161–162, 164–165

even harmonics 149, 161

exciter 161

expander 77–78, 160–161

expansion 5, 78–81

Facebook 49, 106, 135–137

fades 31, 85, 88, 91, 95, 100–101, 114, 152, 172, 191

fading out repeating sections 96
fan clubs 107
Fantagraphic Books 111
far-field monitors 14
Fast Fourier Transform 149–150
fast rolloff 21
festivals 107
file management 97
file naming 18, 48, 97
file workspace 52
file-name conventions 48
file-name extension 48
filters 21–22, 158–159, 162
flat 10–11, 15, 21, 23, 65, 158, 162, 164
flattening procedure 11
flattening the room 10, 11–14
flipbook 23–24
force sensing resistor (FSR) 156
forensics 1, 65, 111
four-foot forks 133
Fourier transform 149–150
frequency 2–7, 10–11, 14–16, 20–22, 25–27, 29, 58, 60, 62–65, 67, 73–74, 76–78, 85, 142, 144, 148–149, 152, 154, 157–159, 161–163, 165–166, 171–172
frequency domain 25–25, 60
frequency processors 159, 161
frequency range 5–6, 16, 21, 27, 62,64–65, 73, 77–78, 85–86, 152, 158–159, 162–163, 172
frequency response 10–11, 14–15, 152, 158, 172
fundamentals of audio 139

gain staging 4
gain structure 43–44, 58
genealogy transcriptions 111
ghostbusters 21
golden poverty 131, 134
graphic EQ 162
graphic fade 91, 93–95

harmonic content 148
harmonics 29, 149–150, 152, 161, 165, 171

Harry Nyquist 20
headroom 4, 29, 58, 66, 166
hearing systems 27, 139
Hellotxt.com 137
high schools and colleges 106
high-frequency 2, 11, 20, 73, 85, 152, 163, 171
highpass filter 4, 57, 60, 158
hip-hop 1, 26, 55–56
horror stories 32
hot apple pie on the windowsill 136
human lens 97

independent music labels 107
induction 154
inductors 153, 157–158
information 1–2, 16, 27, 39, 41, 47, 52, 70, 84, 124, 128, 130, 136, 149, 189–190
instrumental version 39, 55
intelligibility 78
Internet dropbox 125
invoicing 131
ISRC (International Standard Recording Code) 101

jitter 22, 24
Joseph Fourier 149

LinEQ Lowband 57–58, 60–62, 73, 83, 185
LinEQ Lowband filter types 58
LinkedIn 135, 137–138
listening ix, 9–12, 16, 26, 40–41, 44, 46–47, 77, 81, 97, 98–99, 101, 106, 112, 121, 125, 138, 167, 171–172, 190–191
listening for work 106, 112, 138
listening levels 16
Logitech G13 macro gameboard 17
look-ahead limiting 6, 82–83
loudness wars 118
low-frequency energy 4, 65, 171
lowpass filter 21, 158

Mac computer monitors 63
magnetic field 154–155, 157

make-up gain 82–83, 160
MarCard 126, 128
marketing methods 133
master bus 29
master collateral store 136–137
mastering as a business 105, 123
mastering in the box 10
mastering out of the box 3
mastering process 3, 9, 51, 66, 86, 99, 153
Michael Faraday 154
Michael Gerzon Stereo Shuffling article 71
mid-side (M-S) 70
mileage and travel 130
mileage book 130
mixing 9, 19, 24, 25–27, 29, 31, 38, 43, 64–65, 70, 107, 165, 168
mixing for mastering 25, 107
money 18, 25, 105–106, 108, 129, 131, 135
monitor speaker types 14
mono 27, 38, 70–71
mp3 compression 116
mp3s 98, 112, 118
multiband compression 5
multiband compressor 5, 161–163
multidimensional vision 167
MySpace 109–110, 135, 137

near-field monitors 14–15
neutral 6, 66, 69, 71, 76, 140, 172, 191
noise ix, 4–6, 9, 11–12, 31, 52, 54–55, 62–68, 83–85, 89–91, 94–95, 103, 111, 115, 118, 131, 143, 161, 165–166, 172, 186, 189–190
noise colors 11
noise gate 62–67, 161
noise reduction 4, 31, 62–68, 83, 94–95, 131, 161, 186
noise reduction as notch filter 68
noise reduction threshold setting 64
noise shaping 6, 83, 85, 89, 95, 115, 118
noiseprint 31, 62–66, 186

nondisclosure 125
Not Lame Records 108
notch filter 67–68, 73–74, 158, 162–163
Nyquist theorem 20, 22, 24

ocean of air 139
odd harmonics 149, 150, 152, 161
operational amplifier 157
output meter 70, 82

parametric EQ 162
passband 20, 21, 158, 162
payment 41, 131
PayPal 40, 98, 131
personal hourly rate 131
phase 4, 7, 29, 48, 70, 86, 148–149, 164
phase reversal 70
Pho list 128
phono preamp 165
physical mastering 2
pink noise 11–12
potentiometer 155–156
power amplifiers 165–166
preamplifier 2, 158, 164–165
preflight checklist 48
premaster ix, 3, 6, 22–24, 25–27, 29–31, 35, 38, 42, 44–45, 48–49, 51, 58, 65–66, 72, 83, 87, 116, 144, 185, 188–189, 191
premaster transport 48
preprocessing 83
Producers and Engineers Wing 132,
production master CD 46–47, 98, 99, 101
propagation 140, 142
proportional-Q 162

Q or quality factor 158, 161–162
QR codes 128
quantization 6, 19, 22, 23, 83–85, 89
quantization distortion 22, 84–85
quantization genie 23
quantizer 23, 84

Rane Corporation 11, 13, 19, 183
Rane DragNet 13
real-time analyzer 7, 10, 12, 16, 189
real world mastering applications 105
receipt binder 131
receipt book 130
receipts 18, 130–131
red noise 11
register your trade name 129
release 5, 20, 67, 76–78, 106–107, 152, 160
remastering 111
rendering 27
resistors 153, 156
restoration 1, 6, 29, 65, 67, 110–111
retirement 123
reverb 5, 71, 163–164, 171
reverse noise reduction 66
RIAA Curve 2, 165
ribbon mic 70
room EQ 11, 13–14
root-mean-square (RMS) 147, 165
rotation 69, 155

salt 6
sample rate 20–24, 29, 41, 52
sampling 19, 21, 24, 164
saturation 165, 167
Science Daily 128
Seattle Fireworks Audio 112
Seattle to Austin metaphor 84
self-employment 124, 134
sequencing 45–46, 94, 98, 99–101, 103, 107, 110, 132, 152
sequencing workflow 103
shelving EQ 161–162
shuffling 71
sibilance 6, 26, 55, 69, 71–75, 83, 163
sidechain 73, 75
signal processing 6, 10, 13, 20, 85, 159, 161, 164
signal processors 153, 159, 164
signal-to-noise ratio 165
silence 9, 11, 39, 80, 85, 93, 143
sine wave 143–151
Skype 132
slew rate 165

slow rolloff 21
snap game 99–100, 132
social graph 135–136, 169
social networks 105, 110, 121, 135, 137
song order 39, 45–46, 99
song spacing 46
song titles 39, 103
sonogram 73–75, 85, 114–118
Sony CD Architect 99
sound pressure 139–140, 146–147, 154, 156
sound pyramid 26, 27
SoundCloud.com 48
soundstage 4, 69
spacing as a palette cleanser 100
spacing by beat 99
spacing by breath 100
speaker at rest 20, 59, 93–94, 143
speakers 10–15, 27, 47, 56, 59, 152, 154, 159, 164, 166, 171
spectral images 20–21
square wave 84, 149–152
start noise 52, 54–55, 89, 91, 189–190
starting a business 129
status messages 135–137
step function 123
stereo enhancement 4
stereo placement 26–27
stereo shuffler 71
Steve Fisk 38, 183
stopband 158, 162
subwoofer 10–12, 15, 62
summing amplifiers 166
surround sound 15, 25, 78
sustain 152
sweet spot 10–11, 14–15

taking gain 4, 172
talent tarot 134
tape noise 31, 65
teen center studios 107
telemarketers 133
the "cloud" of noise shaping 118
threshold 4, 31, 52–54, 62–66, 73–74, 76–83, 89, 146–147, 159–161, 163, 189
time domain 25, 60

time resolution   22

time-based processors   159, 163

timed comment   49–50

top octave   5, 11, 77–78

tops and tails   87, 95, 152, 172

transformer   155–157

transistor   156–157, 164

transition band   158

transitions   100, 112

tribute album   32, 35, 108–110, 135

truncation   6, 89

tuning the noiseprint   65

TV speaker sound   78

tweeter   11–12, 144, 159

Twitter   135

two-second interval spacing   100

Ultramaximizer   66, 68–69, 71, 76,
      82–83, 114, 118, 187

unity gain   80–81, 164, 166

upper midrange   5, 12, 74, 78–79, 83

valence   154

velocity   148

vertical zoom   91

video monitor   16

vinyl   2, 19, 106, 165

vocal placement   82

vocals   27, 39, 56, 78, 87, 163

voltage   19, 20, 22–23, 147, 154–157,
      163–165

wavelength   11, 27, 148

Waves C4 Multiband Parametric
      Processor   5, 58, 73, 76, 163

Waves PAZ Analyzer   86

Waves S1 Stereo Imager   68

weapon   6, 76, 82, 126, 137

Weedshare   109

white noise   11

YouSendIt.com   48, 98

YouTube   49, 109